Millennialization of Everything

JEREMY K. BALKIN

Copyright © 2017 Jeremy K. Balkin
ISBN-10: 1545065195
ISBN-13: 9781545065198

RMB Books
New York
2017

06/29/2017

Millennialization
of Everything

Praise

"Leadership is *how to be,* not *how to do.*" Millennials truly understand this and Jeremy Balkin makes a powerful case for ethical leadership." - **Frances Hesselbein, CEO of The Frances Hesselbein Leadership Institute, and recipient of the Presidential Medal of Freedom**

"Jeremy Balkin's astute analysis of the significant Millennial influence in deciding both the UK Brexit referendum and US Presidential Election -- he accurately predicted both outcomes (ahead of time) -- is a brilliant reminder that Millennials are a political force to be reckoned with." - **Dr. Emil Pitkin Ph.D., The Wharton School, Founder and CEO, GovPredict**

"Jeremy's work is inspiring, important and speaks to the potential of a generation ready to change the world. He is a role model for young people eager to find new and innovative ways to make a difference." - **Lynn Schusterman, Co-Chair of the Charles and Lynn Schusterman Family Foundation**

"Amid all the controversy and confusion surrounding the Millennial Generation, Jeremy sheds an unrivaled light on Millennials and the indispensable role they will play in the global economy" - **Jon Hartley, Forbes Economics Contributor**

"Jeremy Balkin's TED Talk ignited a global movement. *The Millennialization of Everything* shines light on the exciting path ahead for Millennials and a better world." - **Dr. Shyno Mathew, Ph.D., Curator of TEDxColumbiaEngineering2013**

"Millennials have the power to end poverty with their eternal optimism and entrepreneurial flair. Jeremy truly gets this generation and shares some important insights on how they are impacting the future of business and the global economy." - **Ashish J. Thakkar, Founder Mara Group and Chair, UN Foundation's Global Entrepreneurs Council**

"Millennials understand that Fintech and innovation are a movement focused on destroying legacy systems and legacy attitudes. As we move to a more connected economy leaders are realizing that Millennials hold the keys to the future of their companies' survival." - **Jesse Podell, Managing Director, Startupbootcamp Fintech USA & Co-Founder of New York TechDay Summit**

Dedication

To Rebecca; Mum & Dad; and everyone who believes.

Contents

Acknowledgments

Writing a book is hard. It's the mental equivalent of training to run a marathon. It takes countless hours of discipline and the endurance of pain over many months. Your sleep and social life suffer. I know these feelings all too well because I've run six marathons and written two books.

I never intended to write a second book and it would not have been possible without the unwavering love, loyalty, support, constructive feedback, patience, perseverance, editing and steadfast encouragement of my amazing wife, Rebecca. This book was her idea and she deserves all the credit.

I'd also like to express my deepest gratitude to the many other people who helped bring this project to life. There are thousands of miles between me and my parents, Rosemary and David Balkin, but they're always near in my heart. Thank you for giving me life. I couldn't have better role models or achieved anything without you both. I am eternally grateful for your love, life values, and continued belief in me. Blood is thicker than water.

Thank you to Rachelle and Eric Metzger for their support and enthusiasm throughout this journey. And an extra-special thanks for creating Rebecca.

I want to pay tribute to Pablo Sanchez for being the leader and warrior that he is to me. Winning is a habit and he knows it best. Thanks for everything.

Finally, I want to thank you, the reader. Time is the only thing on Earth you can sell, but can't buy. I'm humbled that you are sharing your precious time with me by reading this book.

Introduction

Millennials are disrupting the status quo in politics, business, banking and financial services, media and communications, dating, retail, transportation, travel and living, and are fast becoming the most impactful generation the world has ever known. In fact, Millennials have changed everything for everyone. This is the *Millennialization of Everything*.

Google the word "Millennial" and you'll find almost 50 million page references. Peppered among them, you will find the words mobile phones, technology and trust, Facebook, President Donald J. Trump, and Brexit. They all have Millennials in common to explain their dominance because the world is effectively being *millennialized* before our very eyes.

Millennials' shared love for technology and innovation explains why there are more mobile phones than people on this planet. It also answers why 87% of Millennials have their mobile phone with them at all times and why Cyber Monday has largely replaced Black Friday, because 50% of all e-commerce revenues will be originated on a mobile device in 2017. Millennials are also the reason 44% of Americans use Facebook as a news source, and that Facebook boasts a population of 1.86 billion people making it the largest "country" on Earth. President Donald J. Trump sits in the White House today and Brexit happened in the United Kingdom because of Millennial voters, or more specifically the millions of apathetic Millennial voters who stayed home.

Millennials' sheer power in numbers is one of the reasons they are creating new trends and transforming entire industries impacting everyone and the world around them in the process. According to Ernst & Young (EY), Millennials will make up 75% of the global workforce by 2025. By that time the United States Census Bureau says Millennials will also comprise 40% of eligible voters. These figures are less than a decade away, but Millennials are already a force to be reckoned with. Consider these current Millennial statistics and their future implications:

- 93% of Millennials have access to the Internet (Nielsen).
- 85% of Millennials use smartphones (Nielsen).

- 87% of Millennials say their phone is with them *all the time* (Zogby Analytics).
- 25% of Millennials consume media via mobile devices (Facebook data).
- 89% of Millennials are active on social media (Nielsen).
- 90% of Millennials only access Facebook on a mobile device (Facebook data).
- 84% of Millennials don't trust traditional advertising methods (Association of National Advertisers).
- 34% of Millennials prefer a brand that uses social media (Association of National Advertisers).
- 70% of Millennials are more inclined to trust what their peers think about a purchasing decision (Association of National Advertisers).
- 71% would rather go to the dentist than listen to banks (2015 Millennial Disruption Index).
- 63% of Millennials don't have a credit card (2016 Bankrate Money Pulse Survey).
- 46% of Millennials trust their employers (EY 2016)

These are eye-opening data points that have, and will, continue to overhaul all major industries. The *Millennialization of Everything* is real and here to stay – but being a Millennial is not purely about birth year. It's an attitude of mind or way of thinking of a person or group. Broken down into five easily digestible sections complemented by graphs and illustrations, *The Millennialization of Everything* clearly outlines the

Millennial Mentality. Parts one and two will help you understand why Millennials are who they are, offering key data points to support the impactful Millennial trends. Part three delves a bit deeper, explaining how Millennials are reshaping the world as we know it, while part four provides 7 Simple Steps for you to effectively motivate and manage Millennials. Part five rounds it all out for you and don't worry, there's also a cheat sheet at the very end.

There are four core reasons why I believe embracing the Millennial Mentality will fundamentally reshape the world as we know it:

1. Millennials possess unbridled energy, boundless optimism, and a can-do attitude.
2. Millennials' inherent entrepreneurial spirit, innovation, resourcefulness, and do-it-yourself posture are infectious beyond their peer group.
3. Millennials fully grasp the enlightened self-interest philosophy, and the responsibility that is associated with it, better than anyone else.
4. Millennials have peak access to the best technology, limitless information, and the ability to travel – and know how to leverage these better than anyone else, ever.

    The *Millennialization of Everything* is deliberately short and easy to read, and will help you win today and position yourself for continued victories over the next decade as Millennials become the world's dominant economic, political, and cultural force.

Millennialisms

Millennial: Person (or people) born between 1980 and 2000; and those who embody the Millennial Mentality and represent the Millennial Modus Operandi (M.O.).

Millennialism: Millennial jargon.

Millennialized: Something that has been profoundly impacted by Millennials.

Millennialization of Everything: the widespread impact of Millennial preferences and choice behavior on all consumers and industries.

Millennialpreneur: Millennial who is an entrepreneur.

Millennial Mentality: a Millennial's way of thinking and their opinions.

Millennial Modus Operandi (M.O.): a particular way of operating or method of doing something, especially one that is characteristic of Millennials.

Millennial Curve: Graphical representation of the equilibrium point at the intersection of the Millennial Mentality and Millennial Modus Operandi (M.O.) curves.

The Millennial Curve

P arts one and two of this book will help you understand the Millennial Mentality and move from point A to point B on The Millennial Curve. Parts three and four will explain how to implement the Millennial Mentality and embody the Millennial M.O. moving from point B to point C on The Millennial Curve. Part five will challenge you to push the curve out even further.

The Millennial Cure: How Millennial are you?

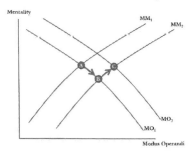

Source: Jeremy K. Balkin

My Confession

" I confess. I'm a Millennial."

Stunned faces and silence filled the boardroom in one of the world's leading corporations, overlooking bustling Times Square in New York City, where Senior Executives and influential decision makers across most major firms and industries gathered over a sumptuous lunch to discuss and better understand the rise of Millennials. No one suspected a Millennial would be sitting among them, least of all me. To their credit, my graying hair and rimless glasses certainly worked to camouflage my aging appearance. At least my wife thinks so.

During the lunch I respectfully sat through a slick, corporate jargon-filled PowerPoint presentation summarizing the research findings about Millennials in the workplace, and waited patiently until virtually every attendee spoke out, venting personal and professional frustrations about these troublesome Millennials. At some point, it felt like Millennials were being described as a virus rather than a group of human beings. That's when I felt compelled to break my silence and contribute a frustrated Millennial's viewpoint to the one-sided discussion of industry leaders and other peers.

The absence of Millennials at the table may be part of the problem. It perpetuates groupthink when it's well documented that diversity of thought is what invariably leads an organization to its best ideas and evidence-based outcomes. Without diversity of thought, which should include Millennial perspective and input, major companies and their executives may never come to fully understand the Millennial generation. Critical decisions based on myths, misinformation and misunderstanding will adversely affect the many individuals and key stakeholders in an organization including shareholders, employees, product designers, marketers, recruiters, and customers.

This experience constantly replays in my head. It confirmed my recurring observation that senior leadership in major corporations, governments, NGOs, and so on, are all rightly thinking about Millennials. Unfortunately, their misinformed opinions have been shaped by weak data, generational confirmation bias and, frankly, a lack of credible evidence to underpin a set of stereotypes. Media outlets also have a tendency to amplify and perpetuate the same with clickbait headlines rather than doing responsible investigation or due diligence to challenge status quo thinking.

In order to combat this and be understood, Millennials have a responsibility to contribute to the broader societal conversation and earn the respect of others through the debate of meaningful words and aligned actions. For industries, leaders, companies, and brands to survive the Millennial takeover, they must adopt the Millennial Mentality before it's too late.

It's about the *Millennialization of Everything*, stupid.

Part I

WHO ARE MILLENNIALS

illennials, sometimes referred to as the Millennial Generation or Generation Y, are the demographic cohort directly following the Baby Boomers and Generation X. There is wide variability as to when this cohort starts and ends. However, Millennials are generally described as those born between January 1, 1980 and December 31, 2000. The term Millennial is based on the idea that the first born in the generation would graduate from high school at the turn of the Millennium in the year 2000. The distinct name is accredited to Neil Howe and his deceased co-author and business partner, William Strauss, in 1989.

Generations are often thought of as a hybrid of birth dates identified by demographers and the significant socioeconomic and historical events that occurred during that time period. Rapid technological advancement, development of the iPhone, innate digital proficiency, the terrorist attacks of September 11, 2001, and financial crisis of 2008 are among the unique experiences that have shaped Millennials and their mentality. This is why their preferences, behaviors, and worldview are vastly different from that of previous generations. The Millennial Mentality has already, and will continue to influence and effectively alter everything from media consumption and purchasing patterns to workplace engagement and political action having a profound impact on the world as we know it.

Births Underlying Each Generation

Number of U.S. births by year and generation

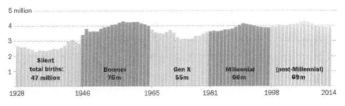

Source: U.S. Dept. of Health and Human Services National Center for Health Statistics

PEW RESEARCH CENTER

Why Millennials Matter - S.P.I.T.T.

SIZE

In 2015, Millennials surpassed Baby Boomers as the largest living generation in the United States. According to the US

Millennialization of Everything

Census Bureau and Goldman Sachs, Millennials weigh in at an astonishing 92 million people, making them the biggest demographic cohort in history. There are no less than 2.5 billion Millennials worldwide. Their sheer power in numbers underscores their importance and means they exert great influence. Demographers and researchers now have every reason to study them. Millennials have quickly become the most heavily scrutinized generation we have ever known.

Studies have been conducted about their likes and dislikes, social media preferences, fashion sense, eating habits, sexual orientation, political and religious views, and workplace behaviors. For every study or survey that's published, it becomes more clear that Millennials are, in fact, full of contradictions and paradoxes. Some of the intergenerational differences will only become clear once the unique characteristics of the next generation become more obviously recognized. Time will tell how this all shapes up. Until then, one thing is for certain. The enormity of the Millennial cohort means they are poised to transform the economy and world as we know it.

Projected population by generation

In millions

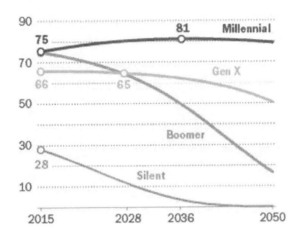

Note: Millennials refers to the population ages 18 to 34 as of 2015.
Source: Pew Research Center tabulations of U.S. Census Bureau population projections released December 2014 and 2015 population estimates

PEW RESEARCH CENTER

PURCHASING POWER

Millennials' peak buying power is decades away, yet Millennials are on the verge of transitioning into their prime spending years. In 2017, Millennials' annual purchasing power is estimated to be $200 billion of direct spending and $500 billion of indirect spending, primarily due to their influence on the spending choices of their mostly Baby Boomer parents. For example, a Millennial son or daughter buys an entry-level 16GB iPhone 6. The Baby Boomer parent sees it and then decides to purchase a more expensive 64GB iPhone 7, plus an iMac and Apple Watch, because they have bigger spending power and want to see what the fuss is about. Perhaps they even want to appear cool to their kids.

It is paramount for marketers to recognize Millennial spending and influence on the spending of their Baby Boomer parents. Marketers would do well to establish relationships with Millennials, as they are an emerging consumer force, and truly understand the Millennial Mentality. After all, Millennials are and will continue to fundamentally reshape the retail space and experience.

INFLUENCE

Leadership is about influence, and Millennial influence is prolific. Leading Millennial influencers who have single-handedly changed the world and its history include Mark Zuckerberg, founder of Facebook; Michael Phelps, the American swimmer and most decorated Olympian ever; Serena Williams, the winner of the most major singles, doubles and mixed doubles titles than any other tennis player; Malala Yousafzai, the youngest ever Nobel Prize laureate; Adele, British singer with the longest-running number-one album by a female solo artist in the history of the United Kingdom and United States album charts; Lionel Messi, considered one of the greatest individual soccer players of all-time; and Usain Bolt, the fastest man alive.

These Millennials, and numerous others, have infinitely more cultural, social, political, and commercial influence than most established elites in business, politics, and the arts. They have transcended their generation and have unparalleled influence that extends beyond their peer group. Leading global brands pay enormous sums of money for their personal and professional endorsement, and the subsequent promotion of products to their millions of devoted followers - in person and on social media.

In this day and age, any athlete, celebrity, company, non-profit, politician, or celebrity wannabe, can announce their unfiltered news to the world on Facebook or Twitter. There is no longer any need for biased media gatekeepers, who unashamedly filter key messages.

TALENT

Millennials make up half the current working population and are set to become 75% of the global workforce by 2025. While Baby Boomer parents have a much later retirement age than previous generations, they are still exiting the workforce at a rapid rate and creating major talent gaps. These talent gaps necessitate the hiring and upskilling of the youngest Millennials in the workforce. In short, if you're not building a marketing plan to recruit, train, and retain the best and brightest Millennials, you will suffer the consequences in future, if not already.

TECHNOLOGY

Millennials are changing the way people shop. In fact, 93% of US Millennials have access to the Internet and turn to their online networks to make purchasing decisions. Millennials have experienced significant breaches of trust during their lifetime leading 70% to trust their peers over other forms of hierarchical authority. Therefore, unsurprisingly, 84% of Millennials do not trust traditional advertising methods. For this reason, the way companies market to and engage with Millennials is more important than ever.

According to the US Millennial Loyalty Survey, 57% of Millennials compare prices in real time on their devices while shopping in a store. This was unthinkable just ten years ago, but price discovery has never been easier and it makes marketplace competition fiercer than ever before. With product information, customer reviews, and global price comparisons at their fingertips, Millennials are turning to brands that can offer maximum convenience at the lowest cost.

Therefore, to turn Millennials into customers, companies should differentiate themselves from their competitors by using customized social media channels and other interactive platforms to engage Millennials. Once companies secure a Millennial customer base, they should acknowledge and integrate Millennials' feedback. This is important because Millennials form intense brand loyalty, and 70% claim they would return time and time again to brands they prefer. More than half of Millennials prefer and make an effort to buy products from companies that support causes they care about. The incessant use of social media by the Millennial Generation suggests that any company, organization, brand, or individual without a social media presence will effectively cease to exist in the future.

Should we actively engage Millennials?

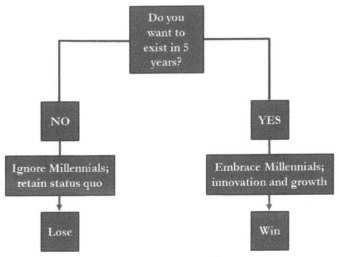

Source: Jeremy K. Balkin

Remember, Millennials are important because of S.P.I.T.T.

Size
Purchasing Power
Influence
Talent
Technology

Case Study – Paul Pogba: The Millennial Influencer

The Manchester United Football Club is a 139 year old professional soccer club based in Manchester, England. They are the most successful English soccer club in history and recognized globally. Manchester United, however, is more than just a winning soccer club with an obsessed global fan base approaching one billion people. According to a report from Brand Finance, Manchester United is worth an estimated $1.2 billion making it the world's most valuable football brand.

Manchester United is a soccer team that also happens to be huge in the Millennial entertainment business. They were quick to recognize the way Millennials revolutionized media consumption via the Internet, smartphones, and social media channels, and diversified their reach accordingly to deliver more content to fans when, where and how they want it. This gave Manchester United greater autonomy over their own media outlets allowing them to control the production, quality, and distribution of proprietary content. With this, Manchester United has built a formidable social media following boasting more than 65 million Facebook fans and 10 million Twitter followers, while its website ManUtd.com attracts more than 5 million unique visitors per month.

This massive digital presence is indispensable. It amplifies Manchester United's global sponsorship value and leverages the star power of their players who are the ambassadors on and off the field for the team. Consider the French soccer player Paul Pogba who played his debut game for Manchester

United Football Club at age 18, and became instantly recognizable to the world. He then left Manchester United for Italy's Juventus who, according to the Euromericas agency, sold no less than 667,000 jerseys with his name adorned on the back in 2015. This made Pogba's jersey the eighth highest seller in the world, leaving Manchester United fans and hierarchy full of regret for losing such a young, valuable player for next to nothing. United then paid a world record transfer fee of $116 million in 2016 for Pogba to return to the club at age 23.

Pogba's popularity, fluency in four languages, charismatic smile, and outlandish hairstyles guarantee him media attention and have helped him personally amass 7.5 million Instagram followers, 5 million Facebook fans, and 2.5 million Twitter followers.

Commercial brands see enormous value in aligning themselves with Manchester United and their players, especially Paul Pogba who is a globally recognized Millennial icon. He just also happens to be one of the most talented soccer players in the world. For these reasons, Pogba is a clear favorite and Millennial soccer icon with unparalleled commercial appeal and global recognition. It's no wonder Manchester United paid a world record transfer fee of for him to return to the team. Deloitte estimates the acquisition of Pogba to be very shrewd, with Manchester United capable of maximizing revenues through his marketability, and legion of young fans following his every move on and off the pitch.

Brands like Adidas and Chevrolet, who are Manchester United jersey sponsors, see players like Pogba as authentic walking billboards for the estimated 700 million Manchester United fans worldwide, who want to emulate their favorite players and hopefully buy the products their idols endorse.

Because of this, Manchester United devised some of the most innovative sponsorship deals and strategic partnerships to unlock the hidden value in their club's brand. United also shares image rights revenue with players to offer Millennial superstar players variable compensation. As a result, Manchester United struck record sponsorship deals with Chevrolet and Adidas. The Adidas kit-supply deal was signed in 2014 and is worth £750 million to Manchester United over ten years. Since 2014, Manchester United's brand value has increased by 63%, with huge commercial windfalls and global revenues guaranteeing sustainable financial success regardless of players' on-field performance. Manchester United has revolutionized the business of sports and understanding Millennials.

Millennialpreneur

Millennials have witnessed great instability in the economy. This spans from extreme market volatility and corporate scandals to the downsizing of their parents' jobs after years of loyal service. The unfavorable market conditions and sluggish economic recovery since the financial crisis drove many Millennials to become entrepreneurs. Some became entrepreneurs by choice while others were driven by necessity. We are experiencing the rise of the *Millennialpreneur,* if you will. Millennials have embraced the startup culture and revived the entrepreneurial spirit that's always been the bedrock of small business and the US economy.

Entrepreneurship is at the core of the Millennial Mentality. According to EY, 88% of Millennials believe hard work is the key factor to getting ahead; 71% believe taking risks and learning to accept failure are pivotal to achieving success. Entrepreneurship and grit are what make the Millennial Mentality unique, in that they are willing to take charge of their own destinies, rather than rely on someone else.

Consider the Millennial college dropout Mark Zuckerberg who, at just 19 years old, launched Facebook from his Harvard dorm room on February 4, 2004. He literally created something from nothing. That "something" has since redefined the way we interact, communicate and consume media. Facebook is now an ecosystem that houses 1.86 billion active monthly users thus housing the largest population on Earth. Mark Zuckerberg is effectively the President of a borderless country bigger than any other, including the big three nations known as China, India, and the United States. Facebook pioneered the social media industry, and its success spawned the creation of other social media channels like Reddit, Instagram, and Snapchat – each of which was also created by a *Millennialpreneur.*

Digital and social media platforms have empowered *Millennialpreneurs* to build new businesses and refurbish others. Morgan Stanley and the Boston Consulting Group estimate that by 2020, Millennials and Generation X will own more than 60% of all small businesses in the US – up from approximately 38% today. The *Millennialization of Everything* is happening right before our eyes and *Millennialpreneurs* are taking over.

Part II

MYTHS, MISUNDERSTANDINGS AND MISCONCEPTIONS

Contrary to the many stereotypes and myths out there, the Millennial generation is fundamentally different from all other generations in history for two primary reasons. It boils down to trust and technology.

Why Millennials Are Different - Trust and Technology

1. TRUST

The terrorist attacks of September 11, 2001, and global conflicts that ensued, delivered a powerful message that personal safety is not guaranteed. The economy later faltered due to problematic economic policy and ethical failures in business, causing the onslaught of the 2008 financial crisis. In a capitalist system, banks are a metaphor for trust and provide a safe haven for people to store their financial resources without the need to cart wheelbarrows of cash and hire private militia. This well-established sense of trust has been at the center of the robust financial system, without question, since the bank runs of the 1930's during the Great Depression. The banking system was unshakable for nearly 80 years. However, trust was the biggest casualty of the 2008 financial crisis.

The events of September 11, 2001, and breakdown of trust brought on by the financial crisis, help explain how Millennials have become such a distrusting generation. However, Millennials' skepticism runs deep and extends to long-standing pillars of society including government, corporations, banks, traditional media, and organized religion. Millennials are therefore described as more cynical, politically apathetic, and less religious than any other age group. This healthy dose of skepticism may explain, in part, their overwhelming preference for innovation and disruptive status quo thinking, as they challenge failed paradigms that have dominated conventional power structures and the idea monopoly for too long.

2. TECHNOLOGY
Millennials are the first generation in history to be raised in a digital, technology and media-saturated world. Often

described as digital natives, they tend to be as fluent in technology as they are in their mother tongue. As digital natives, Millennials were raised in an information-over-loaded environment. Technology has shaped Millennials to be unconsciously "switched on" at all times.

This has benefited Millennials in that they can efficiently perform two or more activities at once. Two human–computer interaction studies at University of California, Irvine and California State University found some indication that Millennials are indeed more likely to multitask than older generations. It is not uncommon for Millennials to frequently switch between tasks and use different media simultaneously. While the benefits of multitasking include increased efficiency, frequent alternation between tasks can also increase cognitive load and mental stress over the long term. There are pros and cons to everything.

We previously explored the role of technology in *Millennialpreneur,* and we'll explore it later on in iCan and the Uber case study.

Innovation

In the *Millennialization of Everything* era, the natural nexus of technology and trust is the unstoppable force of human innovation. According to the EY Millennial Economy National Public Opinion Survey conducted with the Economic Innovation Group, in 2016, 72% of Millennials viewed startups and entrepreneurship as essential for new innovation and job creation in our economy. Fifty one percent of Millennials know someone who has started or worked for a startup; 72% of Millennials consider working for a startup to be a sign of success; and 55% of Millennials believe their generation is more entrepreneurial than previous generations. Millennials are enthusiastic about innovation and using it to disrupt all industries. Innovation and the change it can bring should excite people, not scare them.

Is your organization actively engaging in innovation to disrupt the status quo now before someone else does? It's time to actively engage *Millennialpreneurs* in your organization and give them the bandwidth and resources to work their magic before your competitor poaches them. If you don't, then you will be competing against organizations that are. They will be the winners in the future.

Not All Millennials Are Created Equal

Broad sweeping generalizations and labels have been assigned to the Millennial generation. It's a common but blatant misconception that all Millennials are created equal. Millennials are not one big homogeneous group. Like previous generations, the Millennial generation is a diverse group of people, who come in all shapes and sizes, but happen to be born within years of each other.

When thinking about the Millennial generation, it is helpful to divide them into three sub-groups defined by Bank of America.

1. Younger Millennials

Younger Millennials are anywhere from 18 to 22 years of age, mostly single, and likely to be receiving or finishing an education. Approximately one-third have student loans that they are servicing, and each is a digital native who knows a technology-first world. Millennials in this age range were barely toddlers during the 9/11 terrorist attacks and too young to personally feel the full force of the 2008 financial crisis. They also tend to ask their parents for financial advice and sometimes financial support.

2. Middle Millennials

Middle Millennials are typically 23 to 29 years old, and are evenly split between the single and married status. They felt the brunt of the 2008 financial crisis with many losing their jobs and going back to school taking on additional debt. More than half of Middle Millennials went through higher education and have delayed marriage or family planning to pay off their student loans. Because of financial constraints, Millennials in this subset are also more likely to be on a tight budget than any other age group. Having been hit the hardest by the financial crisis, some consider Middle Millennials to be a lost decade in terms of economic activity, purchasing decisions and financial priorities. Fortunately, most Middle Millennials are currently described as employed, and have friends who are either underemployed or unemployed.

3. OLDER MILLENNIALS

Older Millennials are 30+ years old. They remember what the world was like before the Internet, email, and smartphones. Older Millennials were entering adulthood at the time of the 9/11 terrorist attacks and in the workforce during the financial crisis. Most in this subset are married and employed. Older Millennials have a tendency to have more money saved than their younger counterparts, and are more likely to be saving for their children's education or own retirement. Half of them have a monthly budget and savings goal, and are likely to seek a wider variety of financial information and advice.

	Alive before mobile phones
	Alive before the Internet
	Adult during 9/11
	Adult during financial crisis
	Alive before social media revolution
	Alive before smartphone dominance

Source: Jeremy K. Balkin. Emoji thanks to Apple iPhone 6s.

Meet Millennials: Steve and Christine

Word of advice: never assume that a Millennial born in 1984 is identical to a Millennial born in 2000. Take Steve and Christine, for example.

Steve

Source: Shutterstock

Steve was born in 1984. He was a teenager and watched people get rich during the dot.com boom. Steve was too young to be drinking from the punchbowl, but old enough to feel the pain of the crash that soon followed. Steve was sitting at his PC while completing his college application when the horrors of 9/11 were brought from the caves of Afghanistan straight into his living room, live through cable TV.

The tragic events of 9/11 also preceded large-scale regional conflicts that spooked world financial markets. Lehman Brothers collapsed, a global economic crisis unfolded, and Steve found himself in the middle of it looking for his first entry-level job, after graduating from college. Steve struggled to find meaningful full-time employment and was strapped with student loans he had to pay off. His family was emotionally supportive, but he couldn't ask for financial help because he was worried his father might lose his job. Time passed, but nothing changed for Steve.

Steve quickly became disenchanted with corporations and bureaucratic systems. He felt an overwhelming sense of disappointment in the path his life had taken. He even lost faith in his religion. That is until Barack Obama, the first-term Senator from Chicago, delivered an inspiring and promising message of "hope and change" for America. Steve registered to vote for the first time to elect President Obama, who he thought would restore confidence, better the economy, and improve the overall quality of life.

Feeling reinvigorated by Obama's winning message, Steve decided to borrow his parents' car to drive for a new startup rideshare company called Uber. This allowed him to make some money to pay off loan obligations and have a bit of fun while he continued searching for a more stable full-time job, as the economy hopefully recovered. Until then, Steve feels he can't commit to his long-term girlfriend Laura.

Contrast Steve with Christine, who was born in 2000. As Christine was starting to walk and talk, her parents were deeply worried about the world she would soon experience. They struggled to comprehend global terrorism dominating the 24/7 TV news cycle. Christine's uncle was then deployed overseas for active military duty and her father's work hours were scaled back as the financial crisis hit.

Christine often overheard her mother stressing over the mortgage payments, which were getting harder and harder to meet, and crying that they might soon lose their home. Her mother and father worked extra jobs to make ends meet during this time. Then, when Christine started high school, she began working at the local ice cream shop. She earned a weekly paycheck, but instead of offering to help her family with the house payments, she purchased a brand new iPhone. Christine had different priorities.

Christine
Source: Shutterstock

Christine became completely immersed in a technological world. She's never used a landline telephone, doesn't know what life was like before the Internet, and can't imagine life without free Wi-Fi. Christine learned two languages online and has many Internet friends, who she has never actually met but communicates with daily on a variety of social media channels in the digital world. In the physical world, where Christine actually lives, she has many friends with parents born overseas, who eat exotic foods and have a different skin color. Christine even has friends with two dads. In Christine's mind, she is no different from anyone else. She felt this way in real life, but also online where technology acted as an equalizer.

Christine and her peers grew up in a technology-first world. Her love of the Internet, her iPhone, and its social media applications sparked a greater interest in coding. She learned to code in high school and now dreams of working at Google or Facebook. Christine is now deciding whether to take on student debt to attend a four year college or enroll in a free online coding course. She opted for the online code camp.

Conventional wisdom and research on Millennials would have you incorrectly believe that Steve and Christine think, talk, and act the same because they are from one big homogeneous cohort. However, there is notable variation among Millennials. In the case of Steve and Christine, both lived through large-scale and impactful historical events, but the effects of these events on their upbringing varied by degree. Christine's later birth year of 2000 means she is getting ready to graduate high school, and will largely avoid the same economic pain Steve endured throughout the financial crisis and slow economic recovery.

Steve and Christine also grew up with different kinds of technology. Steve used a slow PC hardwired to an even slower Internet connection and Christine had a high speed Wi-Fi capable smartphone with access to thousands of applications. Steve went to college and earned a traditional degree whereas Christine took a different path and learned coding online. Despite being Millennials, societal norms and historical events molded Steve and Christine and their lives differently.

To avoid gross generalizations and any future confusion, it's best to split Millennials into the three sub-groups previously mentioned: older, middle, and younger Millennials. As older Millennials mature through life, they will carry elements of their generational influence forward with them.

This will have a trickledown effect as the generational influence of older Millennials makes a lasting impression on their middle and younger cohorts, as well as the larger society. Always remember the Golden Rule: "do unto others as you would have them do unto you."

Stereotypes

Many of you picked up this book excited to learn about the Millennial generation and understand their unique characteristics so that you can better engage, motivate, and empower them in your household, sports or business team, startup, for-profit company or nonprofit organization, political action committee, and the wider community. Yet there are also countless individuals who are sick and tired of hearing the term Millennials and have had enough of the Millennial attention.

Skeptics such as these believe Millennials are best seen and not heard and likely think they should pipe-down, put their selfie sticks away, grow up, and then toughen up, snowflake. As a consequence, there is an abundance of misinformation and myriad of stereotypes that have surfaced. Millennials are often and inaccurately labeled as lazy, entitled, disloyal, selfish, and liberal.

These stereotypes are incorrectly shaping key decisions being made in relation to this critical demographic, and have ultimately sullied the Millennial brand. Because the Millennial brand has been so badly tarnished, the Pew Research Center says only 40% of Millennials self-identify with their peer group. It's imperative that we look at the evidence to debunk these widely held, but false, beliefs about the Millennial generation, in order to better understand and interact with them.

LAZY

Millennials tend to be regarded as lazy or not hard working. The stereotypical caricature of the Millennial worker is a cartoon image of an entitled recipient of multiple participation awards, who is unfamiliar with the requisite discipline and sacrifice that comes with hard work. Millennials are often accused of not paying their dues at work and being more interested in corporate perks like flextime, beer carts, Bring Your Dog To Work Day, and summer Fridays.

Not so, says the *Harvard Business Review* citing a study that found Millennials are less likely to use all their vacation days, and more likely to see themselves as "work martyrs" than older workers. The report found that 43% of Millennials proudly consider themselves "work martyrs," and 48% actually want their bosses to see them as such. Interestingly, 35% of Millennials think being viewed as a "work martyr" by colleagues is a benefit, precisely because it negates the negative stereotype that their generation is lazy. According to data from EY, 78% of Millennials are part of a dual-career couple and 47% of Millennials say their work hours have increased in the last five years. These figures hardly resemble the laziness that has become synonymous with Millennials.

ENTITLED

Millennials are often perceived as and criticized for expecting privileges in the workplace without having earned them. There may be some truth to this in that Millennials don't espouse the concept of corporate loyalty. It's difficult to fault them for this having seen their friends summarily laid off from jobs and large corporations disposing of their parents' after decades of service, especially during times of economic uncertainty. This may also help explain why Millennials are not necessarily seeking a life-long career, but are forward thinking and want to take full advantage of whatever perks and professional development their current employer has to offer.

Some might characterize this as entitlement and frown upon it. Others might think: "use it, or lose it." Millennials, however, are less entitled than they are simply disengaged. Millennials frequently change jobs because they are seeking meaningful and rewarding work to satisfy their greater sense of self. A recent survey by Deloitte indicates that six out of ten Millennial respondents chose to work at a specific company because of a sense of purpose. Companies big and small who don't provide their Millennial employees with a clear vision or purpose risk losing them to a competitor who does.

Keeping your Millennial workforce motivated and productive means allocating your own time and energy to empowering them.

This can be achieved by stressing how each member contributes to the company's overall success and praising their individual efforts rather than those of senior managers or broader team accomplishments.

Disloyal

Human resource professionals are often found lamenting that Millennials have little corporate loyalty and are a constant flight risk, giving them every reason not to invest in the training and professional development of their Millennial employees. This is an erroneous belief and thought process that fails to recognize Millennials as the next leadership talent pool.

Millennials certainly aren't as disloyal as they are made out to be. In fact, ramifications of the financial crisis, the rising cost of living, mounting student loans, and higher real unemployment rates collectively point to increased Millennial loyalty through desired stability. Bentley University's PreparedU Project conducted a US-wide study of Millennials and found that 80% say they'll stay with four or less companies throughout their career. Moreover, 36% of Millennials say they expect to stay in their current job for three to five years, and 16% of Millennials say they expect to stay with their company for their entire career. Millennials predilection for stability makes them loyal employees, who will invest copious amounts of time and energy into their work. Millennials' willingness to pour themselves into their work is a definite strength. Their diverse experiences often lead way to the fresh ideas needed to explore new markets and grow existing ones. The hope is that employers will invest in them in return.

Embracing Millennials as the future leaders in the workplace, and exposing them to leadership and career development opportunities, are the keys to current and future revenue growth. Without this, companies of all sizes and industries risk Millennials' premature departure - but it certainly isn't because they are disloyal. Remember, loyalty is also a two-way street.

Selfish

Millennials are often thought of as the generation that gave rise to the infamous selfie picture. They must automatically be all about themselves, right? Millennials are repeatedly described as narcissistic, self-absorbed, and selfish. According to the Reason-Rupe Millennial poll conducted with Princeton Survey Research Associates International in 2014, 71% of Americans describe Millennials as "selfish."

Critics cite that Millennials donate less time and money to charitable causes than any other age group. More specifically, Millennials make up only 11% of traditional charitable giving. However, there are two logical reasons for this. First, Millennials are entering the workforce during a weak and changing economy, have lower disposable income, and less discretionary time. Second, Millennials just give of their time and money differently. It's not that Millennials aren't giving, but rather that they are single-handedly revolutionizing the concept of giving through concepts like crowdfunding.

Millennials are currently driving the crowdfunding movement and rapidly disrupting charitable giving in the United States. Crowdfunding is wildly popular because it seamlessly merges with the Millennial lifestyle and their preference for technology. It is estimated that eight out of ten crowdfunding donations are made via mobile payment or apps, and that campaigns are largely driven by social media networks. At present, Millennials make up 33% of donations on cause-based crowdfunding websites such as YouCaring and Patreon.

Charitable giving often extends beyond monetary donations for the Millennial generation. Some Millennials want to know they are making a difference and prefer more direct involvement in a cause or project. It's not uncommon to see Millennials post pictures on social media of themselves building a school structure in Ecuador or fighting poverty in Africa. While it's easy to see this behavior as vain or selfish, it's a natural way for Millennials to share an experience, amplify a message, and connect others in hopes that it will inspire more people to get involved. Sharing is caring and the opposite of being selfish.

LIBERAL

In 2016, *The Atlantic* published an article titled "The Liberal Millennial Revolution." It explained that Millennials are ripe for socialism because, according to Gallup, up to 70% of young Americans favor wealth redistribution. However, this perception that all Millennials are left-leaning socialists waiting for a Robin Hood-style government handout doesn't hold true.

The Millennial Economy National Public Opinion Survey conducted by EY and the Economic Innovation Group in 2016 revealed that 47% of Millennials consider themselves independents; 35% consider themselves liberal on social issues; and just 22% consider themselves liberal on economic issues. These numbers don't indicate the liberal political bias the *Atlantic* article suggests.

Moreover, research shows Millennials are apt to be politically independent and apathetic. According to Thomson Reuters, young Americans have tended to vote at rates lower than their elders for the last half century. A recent Reuters Ipsos tracking poll also indicates that approximately 52% of Millennials were certain, or almost certain, to vote in the 2016 US Presidential Election. In other words, nearly half of American Millennials are completely and politically disengaged. This decline in enthusiasm is deeply concerning given that the Millennial voting bloc is as large as that of the Baby Boomers and, according to Pew Research Center, will surpass them in size by 2020.

Media, politicians, and business leaders fuel these oft-repeated stereotypes and perpetuate incorrect assumptions about the Millennial generation. If this misconception and disconnect continues to define our understanding of

Millennials, we will see many organizations become irrelevant in the near future by making bad decisions without understanding the facts or misreading the trends. The next time you hear one of these stereotypes, don't judge a book by its cover.

Consider what lies beneath the surface by looking at the flip side of these myths. For example,

- Lazy: Millennials efficiently use technology to accomplish more in less time.
- Entitled: It's hard for Millennials to feel entitled when they have inherited such a terrible economic climate.
- Disloyal: Millennials tend to make more conservative decisions in hopes of stability.
- Selfish: Millennials have been forced to become more self-reliant, but love to collaborate and crowdsource a solution.
- Liberal: Millennials tend to be politically independent and apathetic.

The stereotypes described herein are not widely accepted by Millennials themselves. According to the Pew Research Center, only 8% of Millennials agree that their generational label is a good fit. This is in contrast to other generations, who tend to agree with their generational stereotypes in substantially higher numbers. It's unsurprising that Millennials are fed up with this misinformation and the reputational slur damaging their generational brand.

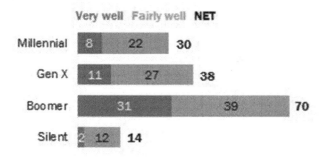

Large Majority of Boomers Say Their Generational Label Is a Good Fit

% of each who say their generation label applies to themselves ...

Very well Fairly well **NET**

Millennial	8 / 22	30
Gen X	11 / 27	38
Boomer	31 / 39	70
Silent	2 / 12	14

American Trends Panel (wave 10). Survey conducted Mar 10-Apr 6, 2015. Based on total.

PEW RESEARCH CENTER

Intergenerational Envy

George Orwell said, in a review for *Poetry Quarterly*, Winter 1945, "Each generation imagines itself to be more intelligent than the one that went before it, and wiser than the one that comes after it." These words were written over half a century ago, but hold true for Millennials and Baby Boomers today.

In many respects, the Millennial generation has been able to learn from the shortcomings of previous generations and time periods. The technology boom was a gift that allowed

Millennials' digital proficiency and greater efficiency in their lives. Millennials are not chained to their desk or limited by a 9 to 5 work day thanks to email and smartphones. Their skillful use of technology enables them to work remotely and have a flexible schedule. Efficiency through technology and versatile work hours have also freed up time in the day for Millennials to pursue other educational and life interests. Older generations have come to envy Millennial attention, their unique life experience and work opportunities, personal and professional freedom and mobility, and adept use of technology.

This jealousy is a moral hazard of senior executives and leadership who, by and large, are responsible for making key decisions in corporate, government, and media domains. Moral hazard occurs when there is information asymmetry. This is where the risk-taking party or people making decisions know more about their intentions than the party paying the consequences of the risk. More often than not, individuals of an older age profile and who are advanced in the organizational hierarchy make decisions that benefit themselves at the expense of the Millennial generation.

Examples of these self-serving decisions include reducing investment in employee training and leadership development and minimizing opportunities for advancement and promotion that then disincentivizes workers. This may have short-term payoffs for a Baby Boomer CEO today, but beware of the long-term consequences. Long-term costs are disengaged and cynical Millennials distrusting of your company or brand, failure to retain your Millennial workforce, and disruption of your business model or concept by former

Millennial employees. Therefore having a deep understanding of the Millennial Mentality will prevent you from making some of these same mistakes.

Trust 2.0

As previously mentioned, Millennials are skeptical and distrusting of well-established pillars of society including government, banks, and organized religion to name a few. It's impossible to blame the erosion of confidence in these once timeless institutions on any one factor, because it is so widespread. However, the terrorist attacks of September 11, 2001, and financial crisis of 2008 are two of the most haunting contributors to this onset of mistrust.

"Who does not trust enough will not be trusted."

Lao Tzu

The 9/11 terrorist attacks threatened personal safety in a way that was never felt before for many. The government's homeland security broke its implied peacetime promise of protection leaving a wake of distrust and fear. Less than a decade later, the economy began to falter in part due to failed economic policy by gridlocked congress. This along with government overreach into the private lives of its citizens set the stage for distrust in elected officials. The advent of leaked dossiers containing treasure troves of data made public by *WikiLeaks,* exposing government scandal and corruption, has done little to restore any faith in the institution. Instead it feeds the already burning fire. Consequently, the Harvard Institute of Politics shows that congress is distrusted by 82% of Millennials, and three out of four sometimes or never trust the federal government to do the right thing.

In a capitalist system, banks have always been a metaphor for trust. Trust has been the bedrock of a robust and honest banking sector since the bank runs of the 1930s during the Great Depression. This trust existed almost without question until the financial crisis of 2008 and the precipitous fall of Lehman Brothers. The 2008 financial crisis set-off blaring alarm bells, and led the majority of people to rightly question the conventional wisdom that had always underpinned our democratic and financial systems. Millennials' distrust thus extends beyond government to Wall Street and the banks.

According to the Pew Research Center, in 2010 just 35% of Millennials felt banks had a positive impact on society and only 28% believed the same for large corporations. It then stands to follow that 86% of Millennials expressed distrust in or with Wall Street per the Harvard Institute of Politics. This same body of research found that 88% of Millennials say they only sometimes or never trust the press. Millennial distrust is pervasive.

As a result, Millennials avoid interacting with those whom they disagree or do not trust, such as Congress or the media.

1 SocialChorus. "Millennials as Advocates Survey." Survey. July 2013.

Religion is not safe from Millennial skepticism either. Scandals and abuse cases perpetrated in some religious quarters have brought into question the merit and authenticity of organized faith. In 2010, Pew Research cited that 73% of Millennials said churches had a positive impact on the United States, whereas only 55% of Millennials agree with this today. In essence, Millennials' rating of churches and other religious organizations has dipped 18 percentage points. Millennial distrust is on the rise and spreading.

Millennials' trust in the workplace has bottomed out at an all-time low. Research from EY suggests that only 46% of Millennials globally trust their employer. The data interestingly shows that the lowest levels of employer trust are in large advanced economies. Just 38% of Millennials trust their employer in the USA; 33% in the UK; and 21% in Japan. The factors important to determining a Millennial's trust in their employer include fulfilling promises, equitable compensation, and effective communication. This is supported by EY's research which says 67% of Millennials want their employer to deliver on promises,

63% want fair compensation, and 59% want transparent and open communication. Despite suggestions of an economic recovery, 36% of Millennials don't believe they will get a raise or bonus this year, indicating utter dissatisfaction in their employer.

The silver lining of Millennial skepticism and distrust is the birth of an extremely innovative generation. Millennials have a verve for entrepreneurship and innovation, and seek to collaborate and crowdsource disruptive solutions to problems big and small across industries. According to the Intel Innovation Barometer, 86% of Millennials say innovation makes life simpler and 69% say it enhances personal relationships. With benefits like these, it's no wonder Millennials refuse to accept the already broken status quo.

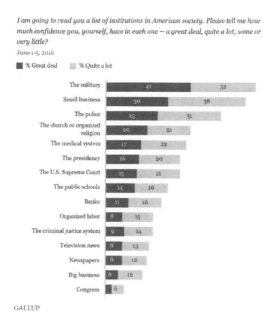

I am going to read you a list of institutions in American society. Please tell me how much confidence you, yourself, have in each one -- a great deal, quite a lot, some or very little?

June 1-5, 2016

■ % Great deal   ▨ % Quite a lot

The military	41 / 32
Small business	30 / 38
The police	25 / 31
The church or organized religion	20 / 21
The medical system	17 / 22
The presidency	16 / 20
The U.S. Supreme Court	15 / 21
The public schools	14 / 16
Banks	11 / 16
Organized labor	8 / 15
The criminal justice system	9 / 14
Television news	8 / 13
Newspapers	8 / 12
Big business	6 / 12
Congress	6

GALLUP

Case Study: Airbnb - Live and Let Live

Millennial innovation and disruption has led to the emergence of companies like Airbnb. Airbnb was born from the ashes of the Lehman Brothers collapse and conceived by a handful of Millennials, who recognized a need for more affordable accommodation in a time of great economic stress. It functions as a peer-to-peer accommodation marketplace that connects hosts or room vendors with travelers via its website and app platform. Airbnb has unlocked excess, idle space in real estate markets across the world and have discovered economic value in an empty apartment or spare bedroom. Airbnb has repositioned itself into a virtual real estate hub and the online hub connects hosts or room vendors with travelers looking for unique and affordable accommodation rates.

Airbnb has disrupted the centuries-old real estate market by discovering economic value in excess and idle space found in residential properties around the world. Airbnb connects hosts or room vendors interested in renting out their empty apartment or spare bedroom for income with travelers seeking to pay a lower price and save on unique accommodations. The vendors and travelers then authenticate one another and establish trustworthiness by linking through Facebook and providing or evaluating written reviews of their experience. If and when a certain level of comfort is achieved, they proceed with the transaction and are charged a service fee. Airbnb collects their fees, Baby Boomers can even monetize their spare rooms to help fund their retirement during this sluggish economic recovery and period of low interest rates, and travelers are no longer at the mercy of rigid and opaque hotel pricing models. Everybody wins.

Airbnb provides hosts or room vendors with an income for their excess space and gives travelers countless convenient and affordable choices in accommodation. It does this all and generates a revenue stream of its own without actually owning any real estate. Airbnb essentially trades on trust between consenting adults in the private free market using technology as an independent arbiter between buyer and seller.

Airbnb isn't alone. Many other companies have also emerged as disruptors. The rideshare service Uber disrupted the taxi industry. Kickstarter gave rise to peer-to-peer fundraising opening the equity capital markets to millions of people. Yelp provided location services based on peer reviews. These are all trust-based network business models that have emerged and thrived in the aftermath of the 2008 financial crisis - a time when trust in longstanding corporate institutions experienced a sharp decline. This may all seem ironic, but Millennials weren't about to put their future in the hands of the very institutions they distrusted. So, with necessity as the mother of invention, they embraced innovation and built game-changing businesses. These very businesses have realized billions of dollars for equity and bondholders, paid government taxes, benefited consumers on the buy and sell side, and offered flexible employment opportunities for everyone to capitalize on.

Case Study: Uber - The Platform of Platforms

Ever hear of Uber? Of course you have. I bet you or someone you know used the Uber app today. Uber first disrupted the transportation industry in 2009 and has since become the largest transportation company known to man. It operates in 450 cities in 73 countries, directly employs 9,000 people, indirectly employs over 1.5 million drivers worldwide, and has a market cap of $70 billion. On average, in any given month, approximately 40 million people use Uber and its drivers collectively cover 1.2 billion miles, roughly 35 times the distance between Earth and Mars. More people earn a paycheck from Uber than any other private sector corporation, except Walmart and McDonald's. Not bad for a transportation company that owns no vehicles and started during an economic crisis.

Uber started as an app to request premium black cars in a few metropolitan areas. Since then it has expanded the service it offers users. Uber now offers transportation and ride-sharing options including UberX, UberXL, UberSelect, UberPOOL, UberSUV, and UberMOTO in locations such as Bangkok, Thailand. Uber's success led to the arrival of numerous competitors in different cities around the world. This increase in competition for private transportation drove down costs that were then passed on to the consumer. With so many new and less expensive choices in transportation, many hold Uber responsible for the collapse in price of taxicab medallions in New York City, which crashed from $1.4 million in 2013 to $250,000 in 2016. These high priced medallions were once considered a safe and nearly guaranteed investment until very recently. This was because taxis were once thought of as a regulated monopoly that thwarted competition in transportation and penalized New Yorkers with higher prices.

Lucky for New Yorkers, they never have to hail another taxi because Uber, Lyft, Gett, Juno, and Via transportation apps are at their fingertips on their personal smartphone. However this may soon change, Uber is now trying to disrupt the very transportation model it pioneered by bringing driverless cars to the road.

Exhibit 2: Share of trips - NYC Yellow Taxi vs. Rideshare App - April 2016 vs. 2015

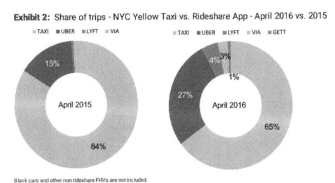

Black cars and other non rideshare FHVs are not included.
Source: New York City Taxi & Limousine Commission, Morgan Stanley Research

Over the past two years Uber has focused on targeting other segments of the transport and logistical supply chain, estimated to be worth $5 - 6 trillion globally. Uber has entered into delivery services giving people what they want, when they want it. Customers can now order sandwiches on UberEATS and request on-demand package delivery with UberRUSH.

So how does Uber change the logistical fabric of cities worldwide with its many businesses? Uber's business models are based on location delivery, payments, and communication.

Application Program Interfaces or APIs are built and configured on handheld mobile devices and then work to seamlessly move people, food, and/or packages from one location to another. Therefore, Uber is essentially a platform of platforms.

Millennials love Uber's ingenuity and value cheap rides, food, and delivery service on-demand. Millennials inspired by business ideas and models like Uber will be the engine of the economy for many decades to come.

Perhaps this growing trust-based economy is working to restore trust in the very things Millennials once distrusted. Currently, 45% of Millennials now believe banks have a positive impact on the country and their evaluation of large corporations has improved, though they remain more negative than positive. Let's continue to build upon the growing trust-based economy and call it Trust 2.0.

iCan

Steve Jobs was the co-founder and CEO of Apple, and is often referenced as one of the most influential leaders of his generation. Though not a Millennial, Steve Jobs embodied Millennial hustle, entrepreneurship, and innovation. He relentlessly followed his passions with little regard for what others thought, and inspired others to do the same. In his famous commencement speech to Stanford's Class of 2005, he advised Millennial graduates to do exactly what they are often criticized for: pursuing their dreams and not settling for less than exactly what they want. "Stay hungry, stay foolish" he famously said. Millennials will always remember this mantra and where they were when they first heard their hero Steve Jobs had sadly passed away.

Millennials have grown up being told by Steve Jobs, their parents, teachers, society, and the media that they can do anything or be anybody they want. As a result, they grew up believing they could always get what they want. Then the realities of life's complexities and a weak economy sunk in and proved otherwise. This line of thinking, and the instant gratification Millennials were accustomed to thanks to life-changing smartphone technology, was suddenly challenged. Millennials have since learned and continue to realize that the very things they want to have or become are achieved through out-of-the-box thinking and hard work. Therefore, Millennials have had to espouse a new "iCan" do attitude.

Thanks to their iCan mentality, Millennials view problems and obstacles as opportunities. They ask themselves *why not*, rather than *why* because they want to source solutions to affect change and reap the rewards, too. Millennials are now leveraging existing technology platforms and bringing new ones to life.

Gone are the days of asymmetric information and opaque talent scouting thanks to YouTube, the online video platform that disrupted video content and distribution circa 2005. Now anyone with a smartphone and iCan attitude can video themselves telling their story or showcasing their talent, and immediately upload for viewers to watch worldwide. Many

Millennials are leveraging YouTube's technology to share their message or talent with others.

In fact, Millennial Canadian singer and songwriter Justin Bieber was discovered after an unknown talent manager found him on YouTube in 2008. He signed a record deal with the agent, released his first album in 2009, and quickly became a global sensation. Bieber's fan base is densely populated with young teenage Millennial girls, affectionately described as "Beliebers." He's sold an estimated 100 million records making him one of the world's best-selling music artists of all time. The rest is history.

Bieber continues to shatter records as he is also the first artist to surpass 10 billion views on the music video hosting website, Vevo. A remarkable achievement when you consider that there are 7 billion people living on Earth today. Bieber's fame, fortune, and influence placed him on *Forbes* list of Top Ten Most Powerful Celebrities.

Many other technology platforms have made their debut since YouTube. Periscope, Twitter, Snapchat, and Instagram are among them. Two Millennials created Instagram, a photo sharing network that has transformed the way Millennials communicate and brand themselves by mapping out their personality and lifestyle in an online photo stream. Before Instagram, personal branding was the sole purview of a celebrity and their publicist. With 600 million active monthly users in December 2016, it is safe to say the favorite Millennial app Instagram is also widely enjoyed across multiple generations.

Bieber and other Millennials, with less name recognition and fewer recognizable accomplishments, who have amassed huge social media followings, are now getting paid significant money to promote company brands and product lines to their fan base. This is a powerful reminder that Millennials can achieve the very things they want in life and more, by harnessing their iCan attitude and sheer self-belief to power their entrepreneurship.

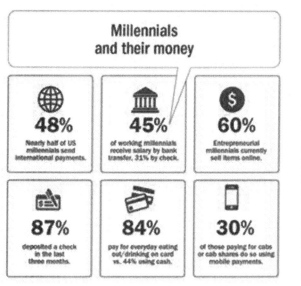

The unique traits and innovative skills of Millennials are not typically sought after or welcomed by the traditional corporate environment, which tends to value more stable qualities and risk-averse experience.

However, companies with forward thinking CEOs and organizational leaders who seek out Millennial employees, for their atypical characteristics and experiences, will find them to be positive internal change agents that use their "intrapreneurial" spirit to disrupt a stale corporate culture. These very companies will surely be rewarded with the competitive advantage they so desperately need to stay relevant.

Part III

Millennials surpassed the Baby Boomers as America's largest living generation in 2015. Their sheer size and unparalleled influence have disrupted the status quo impacting industries all around us. Millennials have already disrupted accommodation and transportation with Airbnb and Uber, the video, music, and entertainment worlds through YouTube and Vevo, and photography by way of Instagram. How will Millennials influence consumption patterns and payment systems that go on to impact the future of banking and investing, insurance, credit cards, and how businesses function in society? At the very least, this section will start a conversation about key trends and how the *Millennialization of Everything* has already influenced the trajectory of our future. It's only the beginning.

The Role of Business in Society

Millennials were indelibly scarred by the global financial crisis that led to an inherent mistrust of traditional institutional authority and power structures, ultimately giving rise to innovative and disruptive new business models in the Trust 2.0 economy. Ten years later, Millennials are expressing a more positive view of business and corporations. According to the Deloitte Millennial Survey of 2016, 73% of Millennials surveyed held business in high regard and felt it positively impacted the larger society. This suggests that Millennials are actually pro-business rather than the popular but misinformed belief that they are anti-business. Though this is uplifting, it isn't the whole story.

After witnessing the corporate greed and excess that fueled the 2008 financial crisis and experiencing the economic and social consequences that followed, Millennials remain wary of businesses and their intentions. The majority, or 54%, of Millennials believe that businesses around the world are profit obsessed and have no ambition other than making money. Profits may be a measure of success for company CEOs and organizational leadership, but the 2016 Deloitte Millennial Survey indicates that 87% of Millennials measure the success of a business in terms of more than just financial performance.

Millennials tend to judge business performance on what a company does (purpose), how it treats its employees and customers, and serves the communities in which it operates. Millennials emphasize the importance of a company's moral compass and deeply value good corporate citizenship and tangible social impact. It's what Millennials expect businesses to strive for and achieve. At this point in time, Deloitte's data shows that 58% of Millennials agree businesses behave ethically and 57% agree that business leaders are committed to helping improve society. However, this perception doesn't always align with the actual impact a business is having on society. In fact, businesses generally have an impact deficit meaning there is still room for improvement.

Work-Life Imbalance

By 2025, Millennials will comprise 75% of the global workforce - but Millennials tend to view traditional workplace rules as senseless, irrelevant and outdated. Their innovative and disruptive out of the box thinking allows them to find easier and more efficient methods and solutions in the workplace. This makes it extremely difficult for Millennials to comply with rules just because "that's how it has always been done." Millennials prefer efficiency and understand that time is money.

Since Millennials aren't ones for needless red tape and bureaucracy in the workplace, it should come as no surprise that they do not want to be chained to their desk during traditional work hours, and nor do they have to be. As digital natives, Millennials are extremely tech savvy. As such, they are comfortable with the concept of a mobile office and accustomed to working from virtually anywhere with Internet access. In addition to working remotely, Millennials want to enjoy flexible work hours that suit their lifestyle or side hustle. Despite this non-traditional work setup, 89% of Millennials say they are "always on" and regularly check work related emails after hours. This heightened level of connectivity demonstrates the technological proficiency Millennials enjoy is actually advantageous for productivity.

When Millennials aren't busy fulfilling the obligations of their day job, they take advantage of a flexible schedule to look for creative ways to derive personal meaning, utilize their diverse talents, or make additional money to pay their student loans and meet the rising cost of living. Millennials often seek to accomplish these things by taking on a side hustle in addition to their full-time job. A side hustle could be anything from a second profession or freelance work to learning a new skill, building an app, pursuing a passion project or writing a book. Having a side hustle is common and normalized among Millennials, who are always busy doing something. In fact, 44% of self-respecting older Millennials have one, as do 39% of middle and younger Millennials according to a survey by CareerBuilder. Companies that encourage Millennials to follow outside interests in the form of a side hustle will be well served by the diverse skill set they acquire and then apply to their day job. There is virtually no doubt that these Millennial preferences and trends will shape the future of the modern workplace for everyone.

COMPENSATION

How do Millennials want to be rewarded for their efforts in the workplace? Most companies think in binaries and assume that a raise or promotions are the only options to offer their Millennial employees. Given these two choices, 77% of Millennials prefer a raise over a promotion per a study from Bentley University. This kind of old fashioned compensation structure is hardly exciting to the spirited Millennial workforce that's driving the future of the economy.

Companies would be better served by implementing or adding dynamic compensation structures including team-based performance metrics, profit sharing, commission programs, and non-monetary rewards like entertainment and restaurant vouchers. These would promote sustainable business growth, increased productivity, and teamwork while rewarding ambitious Millennials with money or valuable goods beyond their contracted salary.

Compensation structures are important things to think about and develop if companies want to attract, retain, and mobilize a Millennial workforce and survive the *Millennialization of Everything.* As the saying goes, "pay peanuts and get monkeys."

Social Media and Information Transparency

For countless decades, journalism and media organizations controlled the news from beginning to end, including reporting, audience experience, and editorial selection. News consumption took place over the radio airwaves and on television. All that has changed now. In 2016, the Pew Research Center reported that 62% of all US adults got their news through social media and 25% of media consumption now takes place through mobile devices. Welcome to a totally new world.

Millennials have revolutionized the dissemination of information and democratized media and communication channels via social media. The evolution and proliferation of social media platforms like Facebook, Twitter, Periscope, Snapchat, and YouTube have changed the way news is delivered and consumed, for the better. With social media outlets at the world's fingertips, everyone can be an eyewitness and share the things they observe happening around them in real-time through a single online post. The beauty of posting to social media is that users feel safe to give a balanced, unfiltered, and unafraid account of what they see, think, or feel.

Demographic profile of social networking site news users

% of news users of each site who are ...

	Facebook	YouTube	Twitter	Instagram	LinkedIn	All U.S. Adults
Male	43%	57%	47%	35%	56%	48%
Female	57	43	53	65	44	52
18-29	31	38	38	58	20	22
30-49	38	30	39	28	46	34
50-64	22	23	19	12	24	26
65+	8	9	3	2	11	19
High school or less	33	34	17	28	8	41
Some college	34	41	38	41	26	31
College degree	33	25	45	31	65	28
White, non-Hispanic	65	55	61	40	65	65
Non-white	34	44	38	57	34	35
Republican	22	21	19	14	23	25
Democrat	31	29	31	40	29	30
Independent	32	31	31	27	34	31

Note: "All U.S. Adults" figures based on non-institutionalized, 18 and older U.S. adults.
Source: Survey conducted Jan. 12-Feb. 8, 2016. Pew Research Center analysis of 2014 American Community Survey (IPUMS).
"News Use Across Social Media Platforms 2016"

PEW RESEARCH CENTER

Commercial newsrooms cannot compete with this information transparency because of constraining editorial bias and corporate interests that influence authenticity and publication timelines. This is one reason Americans' confidence in traditional and mainstream media is slowly eroding. According to Gallup, in 1999, confidence in media peaked to 55% of people across all age groups and has reached a current low of just 40%.

Millennials are also turning away from mainstream media because of the self-inflicted ethical scandals many of the established news organizations have suffered. One scandal involved former *NBC Nightly News* anchor Brian Williams, who in 2015 was caught making false and exaggerated claims of his firsthand accounts of news events, only to later claim he "misremembered." Remember that Millennials value and expect businesses, including media organizations, to practice good ethics. Citizen journalists exposing scandals, corruption, and cover-ups confirmed through email dumps by *WikiLeaks* have only strengthened Millennials' distrust of traditional and mainstream media.

Millennials are now putting their faith in technology companies like Facebook, Google, and Apple, who have disrupted and therefore limited the authority and influence of traditional news outlets. Millennials now rely on these technology companies and associated social media platforms to deliver credible and unbiased information, and there are statistics to prove it. In 2016, 62% of all US adults got their news through social media, per the Pew Research Center's findings. Accordingly, 66% of Facebook users got news from the Facebook's site, which equates to 44% of the general population given that Facebook reaches roughly 67% of US adults. However, it's important to note that Facebook's function isn't limited to news consumption. It can serve another purpose for its users. Consider the fact that Millennials have a median number of 250 Facebook friends with whom information can be shared in just one click of a button. Anything shared has the potential to influence the way their direct contacts and friends of friends consume or choose to vote. Facebook's reach and influence is unparalleled.

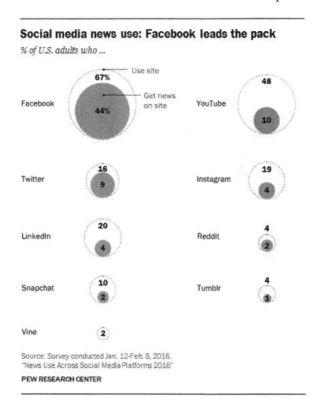

Social media news use: Facebook leads the pack

% of U.S. adults who ...

Source: Survey conducted Jan. 12-Feb. 8, 2016.
"News Use Across Social Media Platforms 2016"
PEW RESEARCH CENTER

Mobility and Freedom

Mobility and freedom are core tenets of the Millennial Mentality. Nothing represents this belief more accurately than mobile devices, smartphones, and tablets. These very things put the world in the palm of your hand and provide on-demand access to information and online content - and no one is more obsessed with these devices than the Millennial generation.

According to Zogby Analytics, the first thing 80% of Millennials do each morning is reach for their smartphones, and 87% of Millennials say their phone never leaves their side. Millennials have come to expect and even depend on having the world and its information at their fingertips wherever they are and whenever they want. Mobile devices, smartphones, and tablets have become an addictive and indispensable extension of the Millennial existence.

Although Millennials are fixated on having access to information on their handheld devices at all times, Zogby Analytics also found that they love the built-in camera. Data indicates that 90% of Millennials capture photos daily or weekly. The study also revealed that Millennials are snapping images of memorable experiences and moments more often than selfies, further debunking the myth that Millennials are selfie-obsessed. These pictures are then readily shared with friends and family across personal social media accounts.

The camera feature of any mobile or smartphone is also Millennials' preferred method of remote data capture to ease their customer experience saving valuable time and effort. For example, they may take a photo of a check for deposit through the banking application on their personal device. Millennials love this kind of seamless transaction and think it takes the pain out of cumbersome and redundant retail customer experiences. That's why 45% of Millennials want to be able to pay their bills by taking a photo, and 33% want to be able to use a photo of their driver's license to enroll in everything from credit cards to gym memberships. Millennials are driving this idea in hopes of greater efficiency.

ADAPTATION

Technology allows for mobility and freedom. Millennials, especially the older Millennial sub-group who knew life before the Internet and smartphones, are constantly adapting and changing the way they interact with new and evolving technology. Remarkably, one in five Millennials are now mobile-only. This means nearly 20% of Millennials exclusively use their smartphone or tablet for email, Internet browsing and purchases, Google searches, social media interactions, and news consumption. Unsurprisingly, Zogby Analytics data reveals that 58% of Millennials have tried to enroll for a new service or account on their mobile and 47% of Millennials access businesses through their mobile device at least once daily. This is why, according to Salesforce Inc., in 2016 mobile accounted for 45.1% of Internet shopping traffic edging out desktop computer traffic at 45% for the first time ever. In 2017, 50% of all e-commerce revenue was earned through a mobile device in the US and roughly 70% of revenues globally, according to Criteo. Given

Millennials' complete use and reliance on mobile devices, 81% believe it's important for retailers to have high quality mobile applications. The importance of a high quality mobile application is further evidenced by the fact that 36% of Millennials have made a purchasing decision or switched companies based on their mobile functionality. Millennials don't just expect a mobile customer experience, they demand it.

These Millennial trends are becoming more mainstream clearly influencing the behavior of other demographic cohorts. Data sourced from Nielsen in 2016 suggests that Baby Boomer parents and other older users tend to prefer a mobile-first social media experience. There is a difference of only 13 percentage points between Millennials and individuals ages 50 and above, who solely use smartphones and tablets for social media. Specifically, 88% of Millennials wholly use smartphones and tablets for their social media time compared to 75% of those aged 50 and above. This is only a marginal difference.

Consumers of all ages prefer this mobile-only lifestyle and are increasing their expectations for more sophisticated, fast, frictionless mobile-first applications to meet their needs across the many aspects of their life. This has had and will continue to have big implications for the desktop and computer industry as well as retailers, financial services, and any brick and mortar concept store. Leaders and businesses who ignore the structural shift in consumer preferences and behaviors will suffer tremendous loss in their customer base and profits only to then become irrelevant and one day defunct. This is the *Millennialization of Everything*, be prepared.

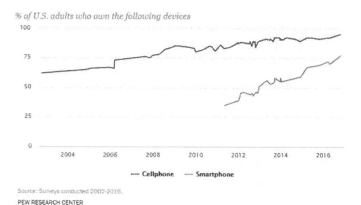

% of U.S. adults who own the following devices

— Cellphone   — Smartphone

Source: Surveys conducted 2002-2016.
PEW RESEARCH CENTER

Mobile also means incorporating virtual reality (VR) and augmented reality (AR) into the mix because both are essential for any comprehensive mobile strategy.

For Millennials, consider:

- 87% say their phone never leaves their side
- 88% have or would deposit a check by snapping a picture
- 60% say in the next five years everything will be done on mobile devices
- 54% would pay using a mobile wallet
- 86% say there are still a lot of websites without good mobile functionality
- 14% wouldn't do business with a company that doesn't have a mobile site or app

Google's report "Micro-moments" provides us with many interesting facts about the way people use their mobile devices:

- 68% of phone users say they check their phone within 15 min of waking up,
- 87% have their smartphone at their side, day and night
- On average people check their phones 150 times per day and spend 177 minutes using them
- 82% of smartphone users say they consult their phone during shopping in a physical location
- 91% of users turn to their phones for ideas in the middle of a task

Zero Marginal Cost Revolution

The Millennial generation enjoys digital fluency and unparalleled access to technology like no other generation has before. New sharing and collaborative practices have arrived with it and the Internet, making it easier and cheaper than ever before for people and companies to share resources and transact with one another. This has led to the reappearance of the *Zero Marginal Cost* concept. The *Zero Marginal Cost* concept describes a situation where an additional unit of something can be produced without increasing the total cost of production. Therefore, producing another unit, whether it's a good, service, or piece of content, can have zero marginal costs when it is considered non-rivalrous, which means that one person can consume the unit without diminishing the ability of others to consume it at the very same time. Essentially, marginal costs for companies are driven to nearly zero allowing them to pass the savings along to their consumers.

The US Bureau of Economic Analysis found the price of software is now 0.7% of its price in 1980. This further indicates the downward trend in technology costs tending towards zero. Driving this downward trend is the Cloud and Internet of Things (IoT).

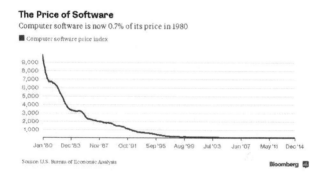

The Price of Software
Computer software is now 0.7% of its price in 1980
■ Computer software price index

Source: U.S. Bureau of Economic Analysis   Bloomberg

Internet of Things and The Cloud

The Internet has enabled the concept of cloud computing. Cloud computing relies on a network of remote servers hosted on the Internet to store, manage, and process data on-demand. The technology and shared storage offers ultimate convenience with no maintenance responsibility, and democratizes access to a superior level.

Gone are the days of heavy photo albums and scrap-books associated with previous generations. Cloud computing allows for instantaneous upload of thousands of pictures to the Internet via iPhoto, Instagram, Facebook, and other platforms. The uploaded pictures are automatically categorized, quickly searchable, easily accessible and shared from anywhere. The Cloud helped Millennials build the largest digital footprint and has set high expectations for music, photos, documents, movies, and personal data on-demand.

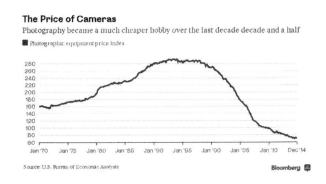

The Price of Cameras
Photography became a much cheaper hobby over the last decade decade and a half
■ Photographic equipment price index

Source: U.S. Bureau of Economic Analysis

Bloomberg

The IoT is a growing network of physical objects that communicate with you and other devices via the Internet. Today, there are approximately 11 billion sensors connecting devices to the IoT. This figure is estimated to grow to 100 trillion connected sensors by 2030. The device embedded sensors will be attached to transportation networks, electricity grids, natural resource deposits, production lines, warehouses, private homes, offices, stores, and vehicles. As a result, almost everyone will have access to the IoT allowing them develop predictive algorithms using big data and analytics. This will increase overall efficiency and productivity and dramatically lower marginal production and distribution costs to almost zero, giving rise to what the World Economic Forum is calling the Fourth Industrial Revolution.

No wonder major corporations like Cisco, IBM, General Electric, and Siemens are building state-of-the-art technology infrastructure to support the growing demand of corporations everywhere, who want to take advantage of new IoT platforms allowing billions of people to connect and share information assets at minimal expense.

It's important to also note that blockchain technology, a distributed ledger platform, will further enable cloud computing and the IoT thereby reducing intermediaries and put an end to the "middle man." This will undoubtedly improve transparency, increase efficiency, strengthen security, and revamp entire industries.

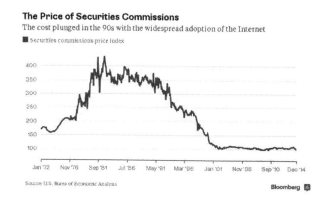

The Price of Securities Commissions
The cost plunged in the 90s with the widespread adoption of the Internet
■ Securities commissions price index

Source: U.S. Bureau of Economic Analysis

Bloomberg

These technologies make it easier and cheaper for people to connect, collaborate and share resources, express themselves, and expand the reach of goods and services. On-demand access to the very things people want and need, without the downside or cost of ownership, yields maximum convenience at the lowest possible cost.

Decentralization of power via the Cloud and the continued use of distributed ledger technology like blockchain will see a world where Millennials continue to question ownership, and existing centralized command and control power structures.

Consumer Behavior and Consumption Patterns

According to FacebookIQ, there are 21.6 million Millennial-led households in the United States, which translates to 17.7% of all US households, and equates to $2 trillion in wealth. In 2014, JP Morgan reported that Millennials accounted for some $600 billion in retail sales, making up 25% of total retail spending in the United States. JP Morgan estimates that Millennials' share of total retail spending will likely grow to 30% by 2020. In other words, Millennials have colossal and impactful spending power. Understanding their spending patterns is critical as it will undoubtedly shape consumer demand and broader economic consumption trends in the decades to come.

EXPERIENCES VS THINGS

Millennials view ownership differently than previous generations, and are buying less and less physical goods or "stuff." They assign greater importance to unique life experiences and are prioritizing experiential consumption. That means Millennials are buying fewer cars and homes, less clothing, and televisions, and more yoga classes, dining experiences, music festival tickets, and travel packages.

This trend is supported by research from JP Morgan stating that in 2015 the average Millennial customer at JP Morgan spent $20,000 on their debit and credit card, and 34% of their spending was on experiential services like travel, dining, and entertainment. In contrast, JP Morgan's non-Millennial customers spent an average of $24,800 and only 28% of this was spent on experiential items. There is no disputing the fact that Millennials prefer to buy experiences over material things. You may even see evidence of their many adventures on their social media photo and video streams.

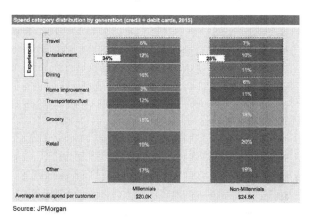

Source: JPMorgan

Millennials have developed an aversion to credit cards and debt since a debt-fueled binge triggered the 2008 financial crisis. According to the 2016 Bankrate Money Pulse Survey, just 33% of adults ages 18 - 29 reported having a credit card, whereas 55% of adults ages 30 - 49 and 62% of adults ages 50 - 64 said the same. Millennials have far fewer credit cards than generations prior.

Besides possessing fewer credit cards, Millennials appear to accumulate less credit card debt. Data from the US Federal Reserve indicates Millennials' share of credit card debt has fallen to its lowest level since 1989; this is the year standardized data collection began.

Per the Survey of Consumer Finances, only 37% of Millennial households in America had credit card debt in 2013. This figure is down by nearly a quarter from immediately before the financial crisis. Overall, US household debt reached $12.29 trillion during the second quarter of 2016, according to the Federal Reserve Bank of New York. These statistics demonstrate the Millennial generation's dislike of credit cards and debt, which is likely to continue - but may have unexpected negative consequences as FacebookIQ reports 30% of Millennials are now unsure how credit cards can even be helpful to them.

Despite all this, credit cards have helped Millennials and other young Americans develop a certain comfort level with credit and debt. This comfort will accompany and benefit them when they're perhaps faced with bigger purchases that require debt financing. However, Millennials are shying away from cash and traditional credit in favor of alternative payment methods including peer-to-peer platforms like Venmo or online payment services such as PayPal. Be ready to accept these new forms of money transfer and payment in this shifting economy.

Banking

Banking and financial services are far from immune to Millennials' disruptive thinking. Chief technologists and management consultants believe banking is at the highest risk of disruption of all major industries. This is because Millennials interact with banks differently than previous generations, if at all. Data from FacebookIQ reveals that in 2016 36% of Millennials preferred to visit a bank branch whereas 49% preferred to interact with their bank via their smartphone or mobile device. According to the Millennial Disruption Index, an alarming one-third of Millennials say they won't need a bank in the future. This startling statistic threatens the very relevance and existence of banks and financial services in the future.

Established banks and financial institutions are facing an existential crisis regarding their future utility. It's easy to blame the excessive regulations imposed on the banking and the financial services industry following the 2008 financial crisis, but it's the absence of innovation and failure to adapt to Millennial consumer preferences that will be their greatest downfall. Banks and financial institutions must not let their sheer size and traditionally conservative ways, making them slow to change, stand in their way. The time for banks and financial institutions to innovate is now.

One third of Millennials are open to switching banks in the next 90 days

Source: First Data © January 2016 The Financial Brand

Traditional retail banks have benefited from customer lethargy over time. However, without innovation, 36% of Millennials say they are likely or very likely to switch their primary bank in the upcoming 12 months per an iQuantifi Survey. Developing a mobile banking platform is a good first step for traditional retail banks, who have yet to enhance their banking technology and services, but time is of the essence considering mobile banking is already trending with Millennials.

According to a 2015 survey by Accenture, 22% of Millennials had signed up for mobile banking apps in the past 12 months compared to just 13% of 33 to 54 year olds and 6% of those 55 and older. A whopping 92% of Millennials make a banking choice based on the digital services offered. Banks' digital offerings are not judged against the digital offerings of competing banks, but rather all digital experiences. Digital functionality is vital to maintaining a Millennial customer base, that expects a beautiful banking app with a seamless customer experience permitting them to bank when, where, and how they choose.

New technology is working to displace the competitive advantage banks and the financial services industry have enjoyed and taken for granted over the last century. However, banks and financial services are slow to embrace technological advancements. Per EY, nearly 60% of Millennials believe government and regulations make it difficult for businesses to succeed. Consequently, many think innovation will only come from the outside. There is a growing belief that technology startups will disrupt and overhaul banking and financial services through financial technology or FinTech, causing numerous banks and financial institutions to disappear.

FinTech

There are currently in excess of 12,000 FinTech companies exploring and actively seeking to disrupt industry areas covering mobile payments, payday loans, peer-to-peer lending, and even financial education. The list is by no means exhaustive and is growing by the day. Despite the heavily regulated banking industry, it is estimated that FinTech companies will capture 17% of banks' revenue by 2023. In fact, 27 privately held FinTech companies have already achieved Unicorn status, each with a valuation over $1 billion and an aggregate valuation of approximately $140 billion. However impressive these figures may be, most FinTech startups have yet to reach their critical mass.

FinTech disruptors need a banking partner to reach critical mass in the short-term. Likewise, the banks need FinTech disruptors and their innovative ideas and technology to stay relevant and capture the massive cohort of Millennial customers. Partnerships between banks and FinTech companies are mutually beneficial and will set new standards requiring competing banks to respond through emulation, partnership, or acquisition. This chain reaction will raise technology standards across the industry in the long term. As the benchmark for technology improves for all banks, the differentiating factor between competing banks will be less about technology and more about delivering a world class customer service experience, which is more difficult for competitors to replicate.

There is no doubt that FinTech will ultimately influence and change banking but, to paraphrase Mark Twain, rumours of the death of retail banking are premature. It is highly unlikely that FinTech will replace banks altogether because of burdensome regulations that have increased barriers to entry, and the incumbent customer behavior of non-Millennials. Collaboration and partnership between banks and FinTech companies is the most probable scenario. If the banking industry gets it right, there will be a unified marketplace that's integrated and working together rather than distinct FinTech and banking sectors competing against one another at present.

Investment, Insurance And Retirement

In the United States, there are 2.6 million mass-affluent Millennial-led households with investable assets between $100,000 and $1 million, and 216,000 affluent Millennial-led households with more than $1 million in assets to invest.

This negates the widely held belief that "Millennials have no money." The truth is Millennials do have assets, but are increasingly concerned about their financial well-being today, tomorrow, and in the years to come.

INVESTMENT AND RETIREMENT

Millennials are faced with a depressed job market, weak economy, and the ever-rising cost of living that make meeting basic standards and fulfilling personal life goals challenging. Many have to make choices about paying off student loans and credit card debt, car and home ownership, and marriage and family. While Millennials must and have to live for the present, they are faced with thoughts about their future self and eventual retirement.

Charles Schwab reported that in 2016 saving enough money for a comfortable retirement was the most common financial stress inducer for people of all ages, including Millennials.

Millennials and young workers share a deeply rooted fear that they aren't saving enough to adequately prepare for retirement. This fear isn't unique to the Millennial generation, but is exacerbated by their increased life expectancy and prospect for weaker investment returns. Having to work and save money over a longer period of time, as compared to previous generations, is a daunting thought for Millennials when economic conditions are less than ideal and they are saddled with so many other financial obligations. Yet, saving for retirement is still a top priority for Millennials.

Millennials quickly learned the importance of taking personal responsibility for their future after the financial crisis, and have experienced an increased sense of self-reliance. Roughly nine out of ten Millennials are taking personal responsibility for their future and relying mostly on themselves to finance their retirement. Although Millennials have the benefit of more time to accumulate retirement savings, data from Charles Schwab revealed that they are putting saving for retirement ahead of job security and more immediate financial obligations like student loans and credit card debt. The emphasis on retirement planning is why having a pension plan and retirement savings account is a "must-have" workplace benefit. Most believe they would also benefit from professional savings, investment, and financial guidance. Companies and their human resource departments offering this are set to attract and hopefully retain Millennial workers.

The Decline in Marriage Among the Young

% married at age 18 to 32, by generation

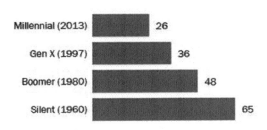

Millennial (2013)	26
Gen X (1997)	36
Boomer (1980)	48
Silent (1960)	65

Source: Data from 1980, 1997 and 2013 are from the March Current Population Survey; 1960 data are from the 1960 Census

PEW RESEARCH CENTER

This said, few issues loom larger for the financial investment advice industry than actively engaging Millennial customers. Deloitte estimates that the wealthiest generation in history, Baby Boomers will transfer approximately $30 trillion in assets to their Millennial children and grandchildren. The Deloitte study confirms empirical data that, in the majority of cases, when wealth passes to another generation the heirs seek to establish their own trusted financial advisory relationship. Deloitte accurately notes Millennials will require a different kind of financial guidance than the Baby Boomers.

Millennials value investment advisors who incorporate the latest digital functionality and advice that also considers the role of investments in society. Being keenly aware of the adverse effects of the 2008 financial crisis on society, Millennials consistently want to consider impact alongside financial returns when choosing investments. Many of these impact investments can be found in illiquid private equity asset classes. Investment advisors interested in engaging Millennial customers would benefit from integrating impact investments into their client portfolios. Over their lifetime, Millennials are likely to gain from a diversified portfolio, with private equity assets uncorrelated to the volatility of traditional stock markets, benefiting their portfolio's performance and desire to impact society.

INSURANCE

Morgan Stanley and BCG estimate that by 2020 Millennials will own more than 60% of small businesses in the United States, which is up from approximately 38% today. Millennials are building small businesses to earn a livelihood, build wealth, and set themselves up for retirement in the long-term. *Millennialpreneurs* and business owners want to protect these very things and are rightly concerned with asset and income protection in the event of distress or an accident. Insurance is the answer, but not in its traditional form.

Millennials are spearheading the reorganization of the insurance industry and digitally underwritten insurance market. InsurTech is described as the use of technology innovations to increase efficiency and squeeze out savings from the existing insurance industry model. The emergence and significance of InsurTech is likened to that of FinTech and its impact on banking and financial services. InsurTech will revolutionize the large and fragmented, but profitable insurance marketplace. Yet, at this early stage of the disruption cycle, only a few traditional commercial insurers are taking advantage of new opportunities to invest in or partner with InsurTech startups. This may be attributed to the high cost and onerous restructuring required by a major insurer to go digital. However, saving time, reducing costs, repositioning for dynamic and growing opportunities, and attracting Millennial consumers are among the rewarding long-term benefits. It will take a critical mass of new entrants and InsurTech players to gather enough momentum before many incumbents start fighting back, but why not be among the firsts?

Politics

Millennials made up one-third of eligible voters in the United States in 2016. This figure is forecast to be 40% in 2020.

Based on this data, major pundits predict that the Millennial generation's political influence will be a deciding force in any 2020 elections. However, their political influence played an unexpected lead role in the United States Presidential Election and United Kingdom Brexit referendum of 2016. This political takeover by the Millennial demographic left nearly every notable pundit in shock and disbelief.

Turnout by Millennials and first-time voters in the 2008 and 2012 elections was higher-than-average, and helped secure key states like Ohio, Florida, and Virginia for President Obama during his two victorious campaigns. In his re-election campaign, President Obama expended great energy campaigning about issues relevant to Millennials including college education, student loan forgiveness, and improving the economy. His efforts paid off, and Millennials went to the polls to vote for "hope and change." In 2012, President Obama won the Millennial vote over Governor Romney by a whopping 23-point margin of 60 to 37.

In 2016, Millennial voters lacked enthusiasm for the two candidates, Hillary Clinton and Donald J. Trump. Hillary Clinton won Millennial voters overall with a national margin of 19 points - but she won Millennial voters by four points less than President Obama did in his 2012 re-election.

Crucially, in the three key swing states, Clinton underperformed President Obama's 2012 Millennial numbers by 5 points in Michigan, 17 points in Pennsylvania, and 20 points in Wisconsin. In two of these states, Clinton's margin among Millennials was lower than her national winning margin of 19 points among Millennials, with a 9-point margin in Pennsylvania and 3-point margin in Wisconsin. Had Millennials voted in the same proportion and party affiliation in those three key swing states as they did for President Obama in 2012, Hillary Clinton would be President today instead of Donald J. Trump.

None of this is to say that President Trump won the 2016 election because of the Millennial vote. In actuality, a comparison of the 2012 and 2016 election results indicates that overall Millennial turnout and vote share, as well as the margin of victory in each state decreased. Both Hillary Clinton and President Trump's campaigns failed to inspire Millennial turnout and voting in the way President Obama's election campaign did. Perhaps this is why we were left with the election result so many did not foresee, and President Trump won the three key swing states of Michigan, Pennsylvania, and Wisconsin, which decided the election result by just 79,646 votes.

To President Trump's credit, he recognized the profound importance and influence of Millennials early on in the campaign. He bucked the trend for employing seasoned campaign veterans, and appointed a number of key Millennial advisers while on the campaign trail and in office. Millennial appointments include Ivanka Trump as assistant to the President, Jared Kushner as senior White House adviser, Hope Hicks as the White House Director of Strategic Communications, Stephen Miller as senior policy adviser, and Ezra Cohen-Watnick as the senior director for intelligence at the National Security Council. These Millennials are each positioned to influence the current Administration and US policy in a huge way.

The 2016 referendum vote to Leave the European Union also surprised the world. In June 2016, British voters opted to Leave the European Union in a vote of 52% to Leave versus 48% to Remain. About 75% of people between the ages of 18 and 24 who were polled wanted to Remain in the European Union. However, being polled does not equate to voting. There was 72% voter turnout overall, but only 36% of Millennials voted, which is why they were overwhelmed by older voting blocs who chose to Leave the European Union.

Contrary to the largely flawed postmortem media coverage, the election and referendum results show that Millennials ultimately decided the 2016 United States Presidential Election and Brexit referendum in the United Kingdom, by *not* turning up to vote. Consider that approximately two-thirds of eligible Millennial voters in the United States showed up to the polls in 2008 compared to approximately one-in-two in 2016. Additionally, only about one-third of Millennials voted in the United Kingdom's referendum, compared to nearly three-quarters of all other eligible voters who showed up to vote. Given the close race in both the United States and United Kingdom, each apathetic and absent Millennial voter made a difference in the final results and outcomes.

With so much at stake, one might ask why Millennials stayed home. For one thing, there was an overwhelming lack of enthusiasm. Millennials who are energized and inspired will turn out en masse to elect a candidate of their choice, like President Obama, or stay home and decide an election by abstention if uninspired, as they did in Brexit. Candidates need to practice authenticity to differentiate themselves and inspire a population that is too young to know or care about a candidate's long history and resume. Secondly, campaigns need to mobilize and use the digital world to their advantage in the way Millennials do.

The popularity and accessibility of Twitter, Snapchat, Instagram, and Facebook have made it easier than ever before for Millennials to have a voice. Millennials use these social media channels to express themselves, politically or otherwise. Clicktivism, or the use of digital media to facilitate social change and activism, is the Millennial version of campaigning door to door, phone banking for a candidate, attending a rally, or standing in line to cast a ballot. This means campaign managers and communication strategists need to adapt to this digital and social media saturated world by delivering key messaging to mobile devices in hopes of getting the attention of a Millennial audience or the message will be lost.

We'll explore this later on in the Case Study – Winning with ABCD Communication.

Part IV

Millennials' unique experiences with the economy, government, and technology have conditioned them to think, interact, and consume differently than their parents and grandparents. Millennials will comprise 75% of the workforce by 2025, but virtually all major corporations, advisory outlets, nonprofit organizations and government entities are led by non-Millennials right now. For this reason, non-Millennial leadership is in a race against the clock to understand Millennial employees, customers, and key stakeholders who are soon poised to become the majority.

The Millennial Mentality is characterized by many things, but purpose and impact are at the core. Purpose and impact are also found in the brands they prefer, products they purchase, politicians they support or elect, and companies at which they want to work. If your organization is built on the pillars of purpose and impact, you are well positioned for Millennial engagement - from attracting Millennial talent to opening Millennial wallets - and can participate in this largely untapped generation of consumers and future leaders.

The challenge is now trying on the Millennial Mentality for yourself to know how to lead and communicate with Millennials in an authentic and meaningful way that will resonate well with them. As digital natives, Millennials source information from a myriad of social media channels so you will have to deliver the right content, at the right time, and on the right mix of platforms to be successful in hiring, managing, and retaining a happy Millennial workforce or growing Millennial market share for your brand and products.

Embracing the Millennial Mentality in 7 Simple Steps

1. ABCD Communication – it's easy as A, B, C, and D.
2. Lead With Purpose – or be a leader without an army.
3. Get a Millennial Mentor – a non-negotiable.
4. Collaborate – or be crushed by the enemy within, or outside.
5. Keep it Real – lead from the heart and empower your people.
6. Ideas Meritocracy – promote innovation and fail to succeed, or you'll succeed to fail.
7. Give and Ask for Feedback – always.

1. ABCD Communication

Effective communication is at the heart of successful leadership, and a skill that needs refining during this time of ongoing technological change. Email and text messaging have freed up time and increased overall efficiency by reducing the need for physical human interaction and face-to-face dialogue. However, this form of digital communication has negatively impacted the effectiveness and authenticity of message delivery for many leaders and organizations.

After previously serving as a digital communications adviser to The Honourable Malcolm Turnbull, Australia's 29th Prime Minister, and Head of Communications in the United States of America for the world's largest retail bank, I have developed and tested what I believe to be a simple, but strong and effective framework for communication. Some might say communication should be as easy as "ABC, 1-2-3 and Do-Re-Mi." Instead, it's as easy as ABC and D. That's why I call this proprietary communications framework, ABCD Communication.

According to the Millennial Leadership Study of 2015, 58% of Millennials think communication is the most important leadership skill. Use ABCD Communication for more impactful communication with your board, employees, voters, shareholders, customers, donors, children, and consumers.

A. Authenticity

Cut out the corporate jargon and political spin in your communication and messaging or risk being fact checked in this hyper-connected world. Millennials are skeptical of corporate speak and value honesty and authenticity in a leader and their communication. Whether you are communicating a positive or negative message, always be upfront. Millennials are far more respecting and responsive to this approach.

B. Brevity
Spoken and written communication must be succinct. In this time poor and on-demand world, attention spans are not what they used to be. You are lucky if the person on the receiving end of your email reads more than the subject line or opening sentence. Be brief and clear to immediately hook your audience.

C. Context
Context is defined as the parts of something spoken or written that immediately precede and follow a word or passage and clarify its meaning. How, when, and why you communicate the message is just as important as its content. Always provide context to maximize the power and impact of the message you are communicating.

D. Digital
In this age of technology, all communication and messaging must be adaptable for digital platforms. This means isolating and paring down key messages to fit 140 characters on Twitter, a short Facebook post, or single sentence that populates after a Google search. According to the Association of National Advertisers (Barkley, SMG, BCG), 34% of Millennials say "I

like that brand more" when the company uses social media. A digital presence has never been more important. Be among the companies who collectively spent $8.3 billion on social media advertising in 2015 or risk being irrelevant.

Case Study – Winning with ABCD Communication

Going into the election campaign, Donald J. Trump had an existing social media following of close to 30 million people or nearly 10% of the total United States population. This meant he didn't have to pay huge sums of money for traditional media, television or rely on journalist editorials full of political bias that would dilute his message. He used his social media platform to speak directly to voters for free, and his four-word campaign slogan "Make America Great Again" spread virally.

President Donald J. Trump's pithy campaign slogan "Make America Great Again" is a powerful example of ABCD Communication. It is authentic, brief, contextualized, and translated easily into digital messaging. This simple but highly effective campaign slogan spurred its own viral hashtag #MakeAmericaGreatAgain that morphed into #MAGA, #MAGA3X, and #TrumpTrain. This messaging was difficult for opposition to argue against and appealed to economically disenfranchised Americans of all ages, including Millennials seeking something better than politics as usual.

Trump's personal understanding and use of Facebook, Twitter, and Instagram, catchy but relevant hashtags, and appointment of Millennial Hope Hicks as his spokesperson and communications strategist helped him digitally engage with voters. According to Google trends analysis, Trump generated three times more interest online than Hillary Clinton and her campaign. He was also the most heavily searched candidate on Google and most frequently mentioned candidate on Facebook, Twitter, and Instagram. Trump's use of social media allowed him a level of direct and unfiltered personal reach that is unprecedented in modern political campaigning, and it undoubtedly played a major role in his surprise and historic victory.

Effective communication is critical to any leaders skill set. Are you using the ABCD Communication framework? How does your messaging align with ABCD Communication? Can you improve upon it?

Remember, it's as easy as A, B, C & D!

Authenticity, Brevity, Context, Digital.

Millennials and Baby Boomers: A Generational Divide in Sources Relied on for Political News

% who got news about politics and government in the previous week from...

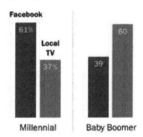

American Trends Panel (wave 1). Survey conducted March 19-April 29, 2014. Q22, Q24A. Based on online adults.

PEW RESEARCH CENTER

2. LEAD WITH PURPOSE

Data shows that 60% of aspiring Millennial leaders want to challenge and inspire their followers with a sense of purpose and excitement in the years to come. So it's time for leadership to set a positive example for their Millennial followers. Therefore, a good leader must have an overarching vision, with reasonable aspirations, for their organization and team's future.

Purpose, or the reason for which something is done or created, is derived from the will to see the vision to fruition. Leaders with a clear sense of purpose are said to be more effective in that they can motivate their Millennial workforce and focus their plan, strategy, and actions to achieve their end goal. Millennials want to feel purposeful and have an impact at their organization and in the world around them. Leading and engaging Millennials with purpose will improve low employee engagement and increase job satisfaction, two major struggles companies face today.

3. GET A MILLENNIAL MENTOR

Historically, a mentor is commonly thought of as an experienced and trusted adviser, who counsels or trains a younger colleague. Many companies expect their senior employees or leadership to mentor the next generation of Millennial workers. Of course, this is a valuable relationship from which a Millennial can learn the informal and nuanced ways a company functions. For example, the mentor may share insights about company culture or politics that the Millennial mentee wouldn't get from a formal training. However, this mentor-mentee relationship can also work in the reverse.

Wise leaders in today's multi-generational work environments should find the right Millennial mentor and take on the role of mentee. The collaborative and information sharing spirit ingrained in Millennials means they are likely to embrace this unconventional mentorship, have purpose beyond their daily job responsibilities, and feel more included in the company's overall mission.

Appointing a Millennial mentor has many other benefits for the leader or mentee. For example, a Millennial mentor can teach new technologies, build a bridge between younger employees and senior leadership, share motivations and concerns relevant to their age group, generate fresh ideas, keep you connected with emerging cultural or digital trends, and show how language is changing for the purpose of a presentation - sales pitch - or business meeting. Now more than ever, it's vital to connect, learn, and mentor across generations and in both directions.

4. COLLABORATE

Sharing information and ideas are at the cornerstone of collaboration. Because of this, it's important for leadership to be inclusive of Millennials. Inviting Millennials into the conversation and decision-making process will help leadership find fresh perspective and innovative solutions to a variety of problems. The spirit of collaboration is all about teamwork not competition. So don't be afraid to learn from and work with another age group or generation than your own.

5. KEEP IT REAL

Millennials keep it real and, as consumers, are more receptive to authentic imagery and slogans used for marketing and branding. Millennials' appreciation for authenticity also speaks to their attraction to social media platforms such as Instagram and Snapchat. Today's leadership must be genuine and lead from the heart in order to connect with Millennial workers.

Leading from the heart helps establish emotional connections and deeper bonds with people. Emotional bonds foster a sense of trust, which increase motivation and performance and contribute to overall satisfaction. Practicing genuine and heartfelt leadership to build emotional connections should be a high priority for leaders. Remember, finding the truth and spotting a fake is only a Google search away.

6. IDEAS MERITOCRACY AND INNOVATION

Millennials' entrepreneurial spirit, innovative thinking, reliance and adroit use of technology have contributed to their ambition as well as their impatience and desire for immediately quantifiable results in this on demand and "insta-world." Millennials see the opportunity for greater efficiency all around them, and are motivated to innovate new systems to disrupt existing business models and industries.

Leadership should accept, and even encourage, this kind of thinking and allow Millennials to critically test the merits of their ideas, products, and services as well as those of their competitors. Cultivating this culture will align with the

Millennial Mentality, thereby accelerating internal innovation and the identification of other markets to which this innovation can be applied.

7. GIVE AND ASK FOR FEEDBACK

Texting, email, social media, and other technologies have fed into the Millennial generation's need for instant gratification. Social media channels allow for instantaneous reaction, response, or commentary causing Millennials to develop a subconscious need for instant and sometimes constant feedback. It's important to be cognizant of this fact when leading and managing Millennials. Be sure to provide meaningful feedback as appropriate. Also ask for their feedback at times, and actively listen to what they have to say. Giving and seeking feedback, advice, and suggestions is a good strategy that demonstrates a leader's engagement, open mindedness and receptivity to new ideas, and collaborative nature.

Part V

Future Millennial Leadership

The future of our world, economy, and all industries will be determined by those who lead it. In the coming years, there will be a widespread exodus of Baby Boomers from their current positions of power and influence in the political, corporate, cultural and media arenas. This will leave a multitude of vacancies for Millennials to fill.

Millennials will take on virtually every leadership role in organizations and industries across the globe, making them the next world leaders. According to the Millennial Leadership Study, 91% of Millennials aspire to be leaders and are excited to join the ranks of already successful Millennial leaders like Mark Zuckerberg of Facebook and Brian Chesky of Airbnb. Others might want to emulate Steve Jobs, who possessed characteristics of and understood the Millennial

Mentality. This may be why Steve Jobs remains one of the most admired leaders by Millennials today, per a survey by the World Economic Forum.

The Millennial generation's enthusiasm for leadership is refreshing, but will yield nothing if 63% say their leadership skills are not currently being developed in a meaningful way. Leaders of today have to look beyond themselves and their misconceptions about Millennials to ingratiate this generation or risk failure in the future. Despite differences in age, experience, views and values, it is their responsibility to encourage personal growth and development among Millennials be they voters, employees, team members, customers or stakeholders.

By leading with heart and purpose, senior executives and leadership will help Millennials become the best version of themselves and create more Millennial leaders. This is desperately needed in a world dominated by social media and fake news where influence and success are measured by total likes, clicks, shares, and followers. The world is full of followers, but scarcely authentic leaders who inspire real leadership.

Those of you who want to win will nurture and strengthen the Millennial leaders of tomorrow, keeping in mind that their most notable traits are different than those of past generations. Interest in collaboration, desiring meaning and purpose from whatever they are doing, valuing social media, wanting real time feedback, believing in systemic innovation, and embracing a flexible work life balance are characteristic of the Millennial Mentality. The *Millennialization of Everything* is real and here to stay. These core traits are to be embraced, cultivated, and leveraged in Millennials who will be the next generation of leadership.

Our future depends on it.

Cheat Sheet

- Millennials are important because of S.P.I.T.T.

Size
Purchasing Power
Influence
Talent
Technology

Take 3-5 minutes to recall important characteristics and preferences associated with Millennials and the Millennial Mentality. Cross reference your list with the one below.

- Millennials are not all equal and can be divided into three sub-groups: younger Millennials, middle Millennials, and older Millennials.
- Millennials are skeptical and distrusting of traditional institutional structures and authorities including corporate conglomerates, government, and media establishments because of socio-economic and historical events that have impacted them.
- Skepticism and distrust make Millennials increasingly self-reliant, not selfish.
- Millennials are not lazy, entitled, disloyal, selfish, or liberal.
- Millennials are politically independent and apathetic.

- Millennials feel government interference and weighty regulations have made it difficult for businesses to succeed.
- Millennials are out of the box thinkers, who challenge the status quo.
- Millennials are innovators and disruptors.
- Millennials are digital natives and live in a mobile-first world. Using technology and social media is second nature to them.
- Millennials see their handheld devices and social media platforms as extensions of themselves.
- Millennials expect mobile functionality in all their digital applications.

Millennialization of Everything

- Millennials snap and post pictures to their social media network as a means of sharing their life, messaging, or cause and in hopes of connecting, inspiring, and involving others.

- Millennials value time saving efficiency.
- Millennials use extra time to pursue personal interests or a side hustle.
- Millennials think their side hustle is as important as their day job.
- Millennials seek meaning and purpose in their job and workplace.
- Millennials gravitate towards atypical work environments that allow for flexible hours and working remotely.
- Millennials want to work for or buy from businesses that practice good ethics and have social impact on their employees, the communities in which they are based, and the larger society.

- Millennials want and respect authenticity.
- Millennials are collaborative and look to crowdsource ideas or solutions.
- Millennials rely on feedback from leadership and peers.
- Millennials are comfortable using peer-to-peer business platforms that are built on trust.

- Millennials are approaching their prime spending years and have massive spending power.

- Millennials practice brand and cause-based loyalty.
- Millennials prioritize and spend on experiences rather than material goods.
- Millennials have an aversion to debt and traditional forms of credit and credit cards. They prefer peer-to-peer money transfer and payment platforms (i.e., PayPal, Venmo etc.)
- Millennials are concerned about their financial well-being and are afraid they aren't saving enough money for retirement.
- Millennials are interested in receiving help with retirement planning and the inclusion of impact investments in their portfolio.

Citations

"Airbnb might finance retirement." Bank of America Merrill Lynch, July 23, 2014. Accessed December 3, 2016. http://www.bizjournals.com/sanfrancisco/blog/2014/07/airbnb-retirement-bank-of-america-merrill-lynch.html

"Annual Report." Manchester United PLC, July 2016. Accessed December 3, 2016. http://ir.manutd.com/financial-information/annual-reports/2016.aspx

"Annual Review of Football." Deloitte, June 2016. Accessed December 3, 2016. https://www2.deloitte.com/content/dam/Deloitte/uk/Documents/sportsbusiness-group/deloitte-uk-annual-review-of-football-finance-2016.pdf

Bacon, Jonathan. "Behavior versus demographics: Why the term 'Millennial' is useless." Marketing Week, September 14,

2016. Accessed December 3, 2016. https://www.marketin-gweek.com/2016/09/14/behavior-versusdemographics-why-the-term-millennial-is-useless/#.V96kGJ8BL4o.twitter

"Barclays Global Financial Services Conference." JP Morgan Chase, September 12, 2016. Accessed December 3, 2016. https://www.jpmorganchase.com/corporate/investor-relations/document/2016-barclays-presentation.pdf

Blake, Aaron. "Yes, you can blame Millennials for Hillary Clinton's loss." *The Washington Post,* December 1, 2016. Accessed December 3, 2016. https://www.washingtonpost.com/news/the-fix/wp/2016/12/02/yes-youcan-blame-millennials-for-hillary-clintons-loss/?utm_term=.1b042bc2a53d

"Born this way." US Millennial Loyalty Survey, 2012. Accessed December 3, 2016. https://www.aimia.com/content/dam/aimiawebsite/CaseStudiesWhitepapersResearch/english/Aimia_GenY_US.pdf

"Bridge the Generational Gap and Win with Plan Sponsors." T. Rowe Price, November 2016. Accessed December 3, 2016. https://www4.troweprice.com/gis/fai/us/en/insights/articles/2016/q1/millennials.html?van=millennials

Bump, Philip. "Donald Trump will be president thanks to 80,000 people in three states." *The Washington Post,* December 1, 2016. Accessed December 3, 2016. https://

www.washingtonpost.com/news/the-fix/wp/2016/12/01/
donald-trump-will-be-president-thanks-to-80000-people-in-
threestates/?tid=sm_tw&utm_term=.ca26e4808fb8

"Confidence in Institutions." Gallup, June 2016. Accessed
December 3, 2016. http://www.gallup.com/poll/1597/
confidence-institutions.aspxhttp://www.gallup.com/
poll/1597/confidence-institutions.aspx

"Confidence in US Election, Views on Democracy." Pew
Research Center, October 27, 2016. Accessed December 3,
2016. http://www.people-press.org/2016/10/27/5-confidence-
in-election-views-of-u-s-democracy/

"Deloitte Millennial Study 2016." Deloitte, 2016. Accessed
December 3, 2016. http://www2.deloitte.com/global/en/
pages/about-deloitte/articles/Millennialsurvey.html

"Future of Technology May Be Determined by Millennial
Malaise, Female Fans and Affluent Data Altruists." Intel
Innovation Barometer, October 17, 2013. Accessed December
3, 2016. https://newsroom.intel.com/news-releases/future-
of-technology-may-be-determined-by-millennial-malaise-
female-fansand-affluent-data-altruists/

Gillespie, Nick. "Millennials Are Selfish and Entitled, and
Helicopter Parents Are to Blame." *Time Magazine*, August 21,
2014. Accessed December 3, 2016. http://time.com/3154186/
millennials-selfish-entitled-helicopter-parenting/

"Global Generations." EY, 2015. Accessed December 3, 2016. http://www.ey.com/Publication/vwLUAssets/EY-global-generations-aglobal-study-on-work-life-challenges-across-generations/$FILE/EY-globalgenerations-a-global-study-on-work-life-challenges-across-generations.pdf

Gonzalez, Victor M.; Harris, Justin; Mark, Gloria. "No Task Left Behind? Examining the Nature of Fragmented Work." Donald Bren School of Information and Computer Science University of California, Irvine, April 2005. Accessed December 3, 2016. http://citeseerx.ist.psu.edu/viewdoc/download?doi=10.1.1.77.7612&rep=rep1&type=pdf

Harty, Declan. "Smartphones Overtake Computers as Top E-Commerce Traffic Source." *Bloomberg*, July 25, 2016. Accessed April 1, 2017. https://www.bloomberg.com/news/articles/2016-07-25/smartphones-overtake-computers-as-top-e-commerce-traffic-source

Helft, Miguel. "How Travis Kalanick Is Building The Ultimate Transportation Machine." *Forbes*, December 14, 2016. Accessed April 1, 2017. https://www.forbes.com/sites/miguelhelft/2016/12/14/how-travis-kalanick-is-building-the-ultimate-transportation-machine/#6fef862d56ab

Hewlett, Sylvia; Kuhl, Joan. "Research: Millennials Can't Afford to Job Hop." *Harvard Business Review*, August 31, 2016. Accessed December 3, 2016. https://hbr.org/2016/08/research-millennials-cant-afford-to-job-hop

Khan, Laeeq. "Trump won thanks to social media." *The Hill*, November 15, 2016. Accessed April 1, 2017. http://thehill. com/blogs/pundits-blog/technology/306175-trump-won-thanks-to-social-media

Kats, Rimma. "It's Not Just Millennials That Tap into Mobile for Social." eMarketer, January 23, 2017. Accessed April 1, 2017. https://www.emarketer.com/Article/Its-Not-Just-Millennials-That-Tap-Mobile-Social/1015091

Kiplinger, Lisa. "Millennials LOVE their smartphones: Deal with it." *USA TODAY,* September 27, 2014. Accessed April 1, 2017. http://www.usatoday.com/story/money/personal-finance/2014/09/27/millennials-love-smartphones-mobile-study/16192777/

Lella, Adam. "Why Are Millennials So Mobile?" ComScore, February 7, 2014. Accessed April 1, 2017. https://www.comscore.com/ita/Insights/Blog/Why-Are-Millennials-So-Mobile

"Millennials and Money." FacebookIQ, January 2016. Accessed December 3, 2016. https://insights.fb.com/2016/01/25/millennials-money-the-unfiltered-journey/

"Millennials and the Future of Banking." CCG Catalyst. Accessed December 3, 2016. https://www.ccg-catalyst.com/millennials-future-banking/

"Millennials and Wealth Management." Deloitte, 2014. Accessed December 3, 2016. https://www2.deloitte.com/content/dam/Deloitte/lu/Documents/financial-services/lu-millennials-wealth-management-trends-challenges-new-clientele-0106205.pdf

"Millennials are top smartphone users." Nielsen, November 15, 2016. Accessed December 3, 2016. http://www.nielsen.com/us/en/insights/news/2016/millennials-are-top-smartphone-users.html

"Millennials at work: reshaping the workplace." Pricewaterhouse Coopers (PwC). Accessed December 3, 2016. https://www.pwc.com/gx/en/managingtomorrows-people/future-of-work/assets/reshaping-the-workplace.pdf

"Millennials at Work." Bentley University, November 11, 2014. Accessed December 3, 2016. http://www.bentley.edu/newsroom/latest-headlines/mindof-millennial

"Millennials Coming of Age." Goldman Sachs, July 2016. Accessed December 3, 2016. http://www.goldmansachs.com/our-thinking/pages/Millennials/

"Millennials Come of Age." Experian, June 2014. Accessed December 3, 2016. https://www.experian.com/assets/marketing-services/reports/ems-cimillennials-come-of-age-wp.pdf

"Millennials Demand More from their Financial Institutions." iQuantifi survey, February 25, 2016. Accessed December 3,

2016. http://iquantifi.com/millennials-demand-more-from-their-financial-institutions/

"Millennials Drive Digital Shift in Small Business Insurance." Morgan Stanley, July 8, 2016. Accessed December 3, 2016. https://www.morganstanley.com/ideas/millennials-insurtech-disruption-in-insurance

"Millennial Online Banking Survey." Morphis, February 24, 2016. Accessed December 3, 2016. http://www.morphis-insights.com/millennial-onlinebanking-survey/

"Millennials overtake Baby Boomers as America's largest generation." Pew Research Center, April 25, 2016. Accessed December 3, 2016. http://www.pewresearch.org/fact-tank/2016/04/25/millennials-overtake-baby-boomers/

"Mobile Fact Sheet." Pew Research Center, January 12, 2017. Accessed April 1, 2017. http://www.pewinternet.org/fact-sheet/mobile/

"Most Millennials Resist the 'Millennial' Label." Pew Research Center, September 3, 2015. Accessed December 3, 2016. http://www.people-press.org/2015/09/03/most-millennials-resist-the-millennial-label/

"Millennials 101." Bank of America Merrill Lynch. Accessed December 3, 2016. https://www.bofaml.com/en-us/content/generation-next-research.html

Piejko, Pawel. "16 mobile market statistics you should know in 2016." DeviceAtlas, April 12, 2016. Accessed April 1, 2017. https://deviceatlas.com/blog/16-mobile-market-statistics-you-should-know-2016

Popper, Nathaniel. "How Millennials Became Spooked by Credit Cards." *The New York Times*, August 14, 2016. Accessed December 3, 2016. http://www.nytimes.com/2016/08/15/business/dealbook/why-millennials-are-in-nohurry-to-take-on-debt.html

Rifkin, Jeremy. "Capitalism is making way for the age of free." *The Guardian*, March 31, 2014. Accessed December 3, 2016. https://www.theguardian.com/commentisfree/2014/mar/31/capitalism-age-of-free-internet-ofthings-economic-shift

"Rock the Vote/USA Today Millennial Poll." Reuters Ipsos, October 31, 2016. Accessed December 3, 2016. http://www.ipsos-na.com/news-polls/pressrelease.aspx?id=7453

Schwab, Klaus. "The Fourth Industrial Revolution." World Economic Forum, January 2016. Accessed December 3, 2016. http://www3.weforum.org/docs/Media/KSC_4IR.pdf

Smith, Justin. "Mobile eCommerce Stats in 2016 and the Future." OuterBox, October 28, 2016. Accessed April 1, 2017. http://www.outerboxdesign.com/web-design-articles/mobile-ecommerce-statistics

"Social Media Update 2016." Pew Research Center, November 11, 2016. Accessed December 3, 2016. http://www.pewinternet.org/2016/11/11/social-media-update-2016/

Somaiya, Ravi; Steel, Emily. "Brian Williams Suspended From NBC for 6 Months Without Pay." *The New York Times*, February 10, 2015. Accessed December 3, 2016. http://www.nytimes.com/2015/02/11/business/media/brian-williams-suspended-by-nbc-news-for-six-months.html

Steverman, Ben. "Millennials Are Freaking Over Retirement – and Not Doing Much About It." *Bloomberg,* August 16, 2016. Accessed December 3, 2016. http://www.bloomberg.com/news/articles/2016-08-16/Millennials-are-freaking-over-retirement-and-not-doing-much-aboutit?utm_content=business&utm_campaign=socialflow-organic&utm_source=twitter&utm_medium=social&cmpid%3D=socialflow-twitter-business

"The Millennial Agenda for the Next President." Harvard Institute of Politics, July 2016. Accessed December 3, 2016. http://iop.harvard.edu/youth-poll/harvard-iop-spring-2016-poll
"The Millennial Conundrum: Save for Retirement or Pay Off Student Loans?" Charles Schwab, February 25, 2016. Accessed December 3, 2016. https://intelligent.schwab.com/public/intelligent/insights/blog/millennialconundrum.html

"The Millennial Disruption Index 2015." Viacom Media, December 2015. Accessed December 3, 2016. http://www.millennialdisruptionindex.com

The Millennial Economy National Public Opinion Survey conducted by EY and Economic Innovation Group in 2016. Accessed December 3, 2016. http://eig.org/wp-content/uploads/2016/09/EY-EIG-Millennial-Poll-Findings.pdf

"The Millennial Economy National Public Opinion Survey." Economic Innovation Group, September 2016. Accessed December 3, 2016. http://eig.org/millennial

"The Reason-Rupe Millennial Poll." Princeton Survey Research Associates International, July 2014. Accessed December 3, 2016. http://reason.com/poll/2014/08/19/65-of-americans-say-millennials-are-enti

Thompson, Derek. "The Liberal Millennial Revolution." *The Atlantic*, February 29, 2016. Accessed December 3, 2016. http://www.theatlantic.com/politics/archive/2016/02/the-liberal-millennial-revolution/470826/

"Traveling with Millennials." Boston Consulting Group, March 18, 2013. Accessed December 3, 2016. https://www.bcgperspectives.com/content/articles/transportation_travel_tourism_consumer_insight_traveling_with_millennials/

"Trust in the Workplace." EY, July 2016. Accessed December 3, 2016. http://www.ey.com/gl/en/about-us/our-people-and-culture/ey-global-study-trust-inthe-workplace

"Two-Thirds of Millennials Disgusted with "Binary Choice" Between Trump & Clinton." Reason, August 14, 2016. Accessed December 3, 2016. http://reason.com/blog/2016/08/14/two-thirds-of-Millennials-disgusted-with

"2013 Survey of Consumer Finances." Federal Reserve Bank of New York. Accessed December 3, 2016. https://www.federalreserve.gov/econresdata/scf/scfindex.htm

"2015 North America Consumer Digital Banking Survey." Accenture. Accessed 3 December 2016. https://www.accenture.com/us-en/~/media/Accenture/Conversion-Assets/Microsites/Documents17/Accenture-2015-North-America-Consumer-Banking-Survey.pdf

"2016 Money Pulse Survey." Bankrate, September 2016. Accessed December 3, 2016. http://www.bankrate.com/finance/credit-cards/moremillennials-say-no-to-credit-cards-1.aspx

About the Author

Jeremy K. Balkin currently serves as the Head of Innovation for North America at one of the world's largest banks based in New York. He is regarded as an international thought-leader on ethics in banking, FinTech innovation, and the strategic engagement of Millennials in financial services.

His first book, *Investing with Impact: Why Finance is a Force for Good* received the Gold Medal for Business Ethics at the 2016 Axiom Business Book Awards (USA) and won the General Business category at the 2016 International Book Awards.

The Huffington Post described Jeremy K. Balkin as the "Anti-Wolf of Wall Street" for his work making the case for ethics in finance. His popular TEDx talk "The Noble Cause", has been viewed over 350,000 times on YouTube, and he is a highly sought after keynote presenter who has been invited to speak at Davos, the United Nations, Harvard Business School, and London School of Economics.

Jeremy K. Balkin

Jeremy K. Balkin is designated a Young Global Leader by the World Economic Forum and selected as a Top 35 Millennial Influencer in the USA for 2017. He has studied at the UNSW Business School and Harvard Kennedy School, and has run six marathons.

Follow Jeremy K. Balkin by searching for @jbapex and #MillennialBook on Twitter and Instagram.

www.MillennializationOfEverything.com

Made in the USA
Middletown, DE
10 June 2017